PRODUCTIZING
LEGAL WORK

PRODUCTIZING LEGAL WORK

Providing Legal Expertise at Scale

Gabriel H. Teninbaum

Assistant Dean of Innovation,
Strategic Initiatives, & Distance Education
Professor of Legal Writing
Suffolk University Law School

Wolters Kluwer

Published by Wolters Kluwer in New York.

Wolters Kluwer Legal & Regulatory U.S. serves customers worldwide with CCH, Aspen Publishers, and Kluwer Law International products. (www.WKLegaledu.com)

To contact Customer Service, e-mail customer.service@wolterskluwer.com, call 1-800-234-1660, fax 1-800-901-9075, or mail correspondence to:

Wolters Kluwer
Attn: Order Department
PO Box 990
Frederick, MD 21705

1 2 3 4 5 6 7 8 9 0

ISBN 978-1-5438-3517-5

Library of Congress Cataloging-in-Publication Data

Names: Teninbaum, Gabriel H., 1976- author.
Title: Productizing legal work : providing legal expertise at scale / Gabriel H. Teninbaum, Assistant Dean of Innovation, Strategic Initiatives, and Distance Education, Professor of Legal Writing, Suffolk University Law School.
Description: New York : Wolters Kluwer, [2022] | Includes bibliographical references and index. | Summary: "Textbook on productization of legal work" — Provided by publisher.
Identifiers: LCCN 2021038460 (print) | LCCN 2021038461 (ebook) | ISBN 9781543835175 (paperback) | ISBN 9781543835182 (ebook)
Subjects: LCSH: Practice of law — United States.
Classification: LCC KF300 .T46 2022 (print) | LCC KF300 (ebook) | DDC 340.068/5 — dc23
LC record available at https://lccn.loc.gov/2021038460
LC ebook record available at https://lccn.loc.gov/2021038461

About Wolters Kluwer Legal & Regulatory U.S.

Wolters Kluwer Legal & Regulatory U.S. delivers expert content and solutions in the areas of law, corporate compliance, health compliance, reimbursement, and legal education. Its practical solutions help customers successfully navigate the demands of a changing environment to drive their daily activities, enhance decision quality and inspire confident outcomes.

Serving customers worldwide, its legal and regulatory portfolio includes products under the Aspen Publishers, CCH Incorporated, Kluwer Law International, ftwilliam.com and MediRegs names. They are regarded as exceptional and trusted resources for general legal and practice-specific knowledge, compliance and risk management, dynamic workflow solutions, and expert commentary.

For my family, especially my wife, Christine, who delivered me motivational cheese to get me through writing this; my children, Annelise and Jonas, who are my favorite products; and my parents, Mark and Shelley, who spent my entire childhood unsuccessfully trying to convince me to read a book and are now stuck reading this one that I wrote.

Summary of Contents

Part I. The Role of Productization in a Changing Legal Industry 1

Part II. A Process for Productizing Legal Work 49

Contents

CHAPTER 2: UNBUNDLING LEGAL WORK   17

CHAPTER 3: PATTERNS OF PRODUCTIZATION   23

Part II. A Process for Productizing Legal Work   49

CHAPTER 4: BEGIN BY ASSESSING YOUR RESOURCES AND GOALS   51

CHAPTER 5: IDENTIFY PROBLEMS, THEN WORK BACKWARD   65

CHAPTER 6: SURVEY THE COMPETITIVE ENVIRONMENT   75

CHAPTER 7: CREATE AND TEST AN ELEVATOR PITCH   83

CHAPTER 8: CREATE A PROTOTYPE   91

CHAPTER 9: SEEK END-USER FEEDBACK—AND ITERATE
BASED ON IT   101

CHAPTER 12: CREATE A MARKETING PLAN FOR LAUNCH 133

CHAPTER 13: LAUNCH ... AND BEYOND! 141

Preface

When I'm not teaching law students about the intersection of legal work, innovation, and technology, another portion of my working life is spent speaking to legal professionals about this same topic. The way it works is pretty straightforward: I give talks at conferences, bar association meetings, and law firm retreats about the power of new processes, tools, and technologies to deliver more value to clients at a lower cost while maximizing an organization's efficiency and profitability.

During these talks, I cite examples of several law firms that have used the process of productization to reimagine their work, as well as companies that have become multi-billion-dollar enterprises using this model. And I offer what I hope will be a tantalizing introduction to how those listening could do likewise by building their own productized services.

When I return to my office from these events, I frequently have emails from attendees who want to know if these ideas will apply to their own organization's work. After some probing, the answer is almost invariably, "Yes, probably." (Over time, I've learned that legal professionals tend to be really good at helping clients solve important problems, but not usually as good at doing so efficiently.) Sometimes, these email exchanges result in a consulting engagement in which I sit face-to-face with an innovation committee or law department's leadership team, and we work together to identify inefficiencies in their process and determine whether a proposed solution for one or more inefficiencies is a good one. Making that determination involves several steps: generating ideas, building prototypes, soliciting feedback, and improving on those prototypes based on that feedback.

A fact that I don't share with these clients, or my audiences at events, is that probably 85% of all conversations I have about productizing legal services are repeated; that is to say, the core concepts don't change, and the examples I cite are fairly consistent. Sometimes there's a new point to make, or some new research to cite, but by and large, each conversation follows a similar script. So, recognizing that redundancy, and viewing it as an inefficiency, I decided to point the lens at my own consulting work and consider productizing my own service. I asked: "Can I, and should I, create a product out of my speaking and consulting services? Would I be able to deliver a similarly good body of information to far more people at a far lower cost if I delivered it in a new format?" After going through the process I teach to students, I determined the answer was "yes." That product is this book.

Ultimately, this is all productization really is: Taking a one-off piece of service work that is done over and over (i.e., giving talks and consulting on productization) and re-packaging it into something that lets more people benefit from its efficiency and far lower cost. That's what I've done by writing a book that captures the lessons I teach and selling it for a fraction of what I charge for a speaking engagement.

I'll still likely do some consulting—unique situations will still arise—but when I do consult, that will change also. Publication of this book means I can have conversations with clients that are more efficient and which start at a higher level. It will also mean that I can focus my energy on helping others reach creative solutions, rather than having to repeat the same spiel over and over about the steps of productization.

Writing about productizing legal work has been challenging and enjoyable. It has allowed me to reconnect with important ideas I've taught to law students in live classes, and it has given me a chance to think about how to best convey those ideas to a broad audience. As you read this book, you'll find many examples of individuals and organizations that have taken this path and, as a result, are better able to serve their clients while improving their own professional success and satisfaction. I hope it inspires and motivates you to engage in thinking about how certain aspects of your own expertise could be scaled.

Acknowledgments

I have benefited from the support, advice, and feedback from lots of knowledgeable and generous people in writing this book. Those people include: Dyane O'Leary, Richard Granat, Marc Lauritsen, Kate Ball, Richard Susskind, Jeff Marple, Dennis Kennedy, Mike Cappucci, Colin Levy, Joe Regalia, Shaun Jamison, and Sarah Schendel.

Thanks to all those who generously shared quotes and anecdotes that are highlighted in the book.

Thanks to my Suffolk Law colleagues: Dean Andy Perlman—a first ballot legal innovation Hall of Famer—and Associate Deans Leah Grinvald and Pat Shin. They were all encouraging of this project and approved the sabbatical time I used to write it. Thanks also to my colleagues working within Suffolk Law's legal tech program, who are a source of constant inspiration: David Colarusso, Quinten Steenhuis, and the aforementioned Dyane O'Leary.

Special thanks to my editing team: Jordan Jepsen, Jessica Barmack, and Lisa Connery, who helped me immensely; and to Nicole Pinard and Joe Terry from Wolters Kluwer for believing in this project.

Thank you to Christine, Annelise, and Jonas for letting me have a few minutes of quiet time to write when we were all cooped up during the pandemic.

Thanks to my parents, Mark and Shelley, the Brandsgaards (Julie, Scott, Phoebe, and Tessa), the Thompsons (Lee and Diane), the Smiths (Lynn, Justin, Lily, and Tyler), the Contois/Nelsons (Jules, Kim, Mark, Ruth, and Dard), Jon Berroya, and Mike Tonsing. All of them regularly asked "How's the book going?," and I appreciated it.

Thank you to everyone who I failed to include here as a result of my faded memory and my own poor record-keeping. I meant no offense by leaving you out, and pledge to include you in the film adaptation.

Finally, thank you to the 2020–21 New England Patriots, whose performance gave me plenty of reasons to turn off the television and get back to work on the book.

The Role of Productization in a Changing Legal Industry

Part I explains what it means to productize a service, exploring the positive and negative impacts of productized services in the legal environment as well as across other industries.

Part I lays the groundwork for the hands-on coverage in Part II, which provides details on how to understand the process and skills involved in productizing legal services.

Chapter 1

Productizing Services: A New Opportunity for a New Time

WHAT DOES IT MEAN TO PRODUCTIZE A SERVICE?

Richard Granat is a family law attorney licensed to practice law in Maryland, though he rarely sets foot in the state.[1] Instead, he runs his practice from his home in Palm Beach Gardens, Florida. A litigator by trade, he also never actually goes to court. While many lawyers work a punishing 12-hour-per-day schedule, Granat's schedule is far lighter—closer to 30 minutes a day. One thing he does have in common with "Big Law" lawyers billing 2,000 hours a year is that his work allows him to make a comfortable living.

Granat's path is not only a story of maximizing the flexibility of his lifestyle. It has also helped him make a difference in the world by serving those who might not historically have been able to afford expert legal advice. In fact, a primary motivation for him is that he has discovered "a method that enables people to solve their legal problems at low cost."[2] His method pays an intellectual dividend for him, too: He is able to focus only on work he considers interesting, having used his technique to make his expertise broadly available

---

1. http://www.abajournal.com/legalrebels/article/internet_obsessive.
2. http://www.abajournal.com/legalrebels/article/rebels_podcast_episode_026.

without his own direct involvement. In turn, he has recaptured time to work on what he chooses.

As different as the conditions of Granat's work are from those of most of his peers, it's the way he's done it that's the most notable. When he assists clients through the divorce process, it is through a system that they interact with "virtually." Rather than meeting clients in person for a traditional consultation, Granat's process is almost completely automated. Clients log onto a website and answer a series of questions generated by a computer program. They fill in information like how many children they have, their separation date, whether they own property, and other questions related to the divorce process. After they have done so, the system uses their information to generate the appropriate court forms for that particular client's situation.

Once the software has done its work, clients can opt for a web-based consultation with Granat or they can continue on their way with instructions on filing the forms. In the end, the clients get the value and level of service that they want to solve their problem. The service is there whenever the clients need it, and moreover, Granat's robotic doppelgänger never sleeps, takes a day off, or makes a mistake because it is distracted.

This is an example of *productization of a service*. Richard Granat has transformed a set of legal tasks that were traditionally provided on a one-to-one basis at an hourly rate and transformed it into a product that can be provided to hundreds of clients simultaneously at a low, fixed cost. To do so, Granat created software programs that ask the types of questions that an attorney would ask a client to assess their situation. Based on the client's responses, the program provides the legal guidance that Granat himself would give to a client in the same set of circumstances. The clients interact with Granat's software, but the legal expertise they receive is the product of Granat's own wealth of experience in legal practice.

What Granat has done is just one of several examples of how productization can make legal work more effective and efficient. In addition to several existing examples of productized legal services aimed at consumers, other productized legal services have arisen in different contexts:

- An attorney creates and sells other lawyers a widely used software program that computes actuarial factors for tax calculations and planning.
- A prominent technology company sought out a law firm to create a document assembly application for standard agreements that the company would license on an annual subscription basis.
- A law firm produces public training videos on legal topics.
- A law firm packages research information updated on an annual basis as a subscription offering.[3]

What these all have in common is that they take work that was historically billed by the hour and leverage technology to scale that work to serve an essentially unlimited number of users at a much lower cost.

Using Productization to Harness Expertise in "Knowledge Industries"

In the winter of 2014, my wife was newly pregnant with our second child. Around dinner time on Christmas Eve while we were visiting her family in Maryland, she started to experience flu-like symptoms. Urgent care clinics had closed for the holiday. Her obstetrician in Boston recommended that we go to the ER. A few frantic minutes later, we found ourselves walking into the emergency room of a major hospital in Bethesda, Maryland, where we were greeted by a nurse's aide holding a tablet computer. She could see that my wife wasn't in obvious, overwhelming distress, so she began asking a series of questions: What was bothering her? Did she have certain symptoms? How long had she been suffering them? After my wife answered a question, the nurse's aide would tap

---

3. These examples are drawn from Dennis Kennedy's seminal 2014 essay, *The "Productization" of Legal Services: Finding New Revenue Sources from Outside Business Models*, available at: https://www.denniskennedy.com/blog/2019/04/productization-of-legal-services-2014-version/.

something into her tablet. Soon, she finished the interview and directed us to a corner of the ER to wait for a doctor.

After my wife had been seen by a physician, diagnosed (it was the flu), and discharged, we stopped by the main desk on the way out so I could ask the nurse's aide about the tablet she had used. She explained to me that the hospital used expert system software that prompted her to ask the same questions that a "live" ER doctor would ask in the course of triaging a patient. On the basis of the patient's answers, which the nurse's aide input into her tablet, the expert system would determine where a patient would go in the triage queue. This is how I learned first-hand how productized services could make medical expertise available to the assisting staff to make health care operate more efficiently and effectively.

And, I'm happy to report, several months later, my wife gave birth to our healthy baby boy.

So, it is not the legal industry alone that is moving toward productizing services. As in the example above, productization is emerging across many "knowledge industries," including medicine, accounting, and technology. For example,

- Internists subscribe to apps that allow them to double-check diagnoses and better educate patients on medications, ailments, and healthy living.
- Accountants use robotic processing automation to help process invoices, thus shifting their own former data entry work to analysis roles.
- Website designers can purchase access to tools and templates that reduce the technical expertise and work required to create a new webpage, so the designer can focus more exclusively on how the page looks.

Using Productization to Expand Market Share or Reach New Audiences

Through productizing, opportunities exist as never before for everyday people to make use of new tools to find a broader audience for their work. YouTube personalities, livestreamers, gamers who narrate their game-play over Twitch, and Instagram celebrities all harness easy-to-use and free technology to spread their message. The reach of such people and their ideas is broader than it has ever been, and it can be accessed with less effort than ever before.

WHAT DOES IT MEAN TO *SCALE* A SERVICE?

In 1909, the Ford Motor Company produced 10,666 of their Model T "Runabouts" at a cost of $825 each. By 1915, Ford made 30 times that many cars — 308,162, to be exact — and at less than half the cost of making a single car in 1909 ($390 as compared to $825). In 1921, Ford more than tripled their 1915 production numbers and dropped costs again by about 20 percent (now $325 each). And by 1925, productivity peaked with 1,911,705 Roundabouts produced at a cost of $260 per car.

Over 16 years, Ford was able to produce almost 200 times as many Runabouts as when they first started in 1909, and at less than one-third of the original unit cost. Ford became fabulously successful, made their product affordable for everyday families, and changed the course of American life. This level of productivity ushered in a new era of freedom and prosperity for everyday people, and promoted the new technology that achieved it.

Ford is a good example of how a process (car production) can be made more efficient for the purpose of increasing productivity and lowering production costs. Paired with new approaches (workers focusing on single tasks) and technologies (the assembly line), the company leveraged a world-changing combination of innovations. As in the example above, the payoff for learning to produce to scale can translate into dramatic change across industries.

WHAT IS THE POTENTIAL FOR PRODUCTIZING LEGAL SERVICES?

In the first example of this chapter, we saw that the number of divorce clients who can access legal expertise through Richard Granat's website is only limited by the bandwidth of his server.

Big law firms can rely on an army of paralegals and associates to perform much of the work that allows the firm to serve numerous clients (though, of course, those costs get passed along to *someone*). But what about small and mid-sized law firms that can't draw on deep reservoirs of human resources? Without productization, the number of clients they can serve is necessarily limited. But with productization, technology can potentially do the work of many paralegals and associates. For example, an automated expert system could gather the same type of information that a paralegal would typically collect and record. Instead of a junior accountant calculating the tax benefits of various business models, a calculator app could do it. And legal work once done in physical offices can now be accomplished through the use of eDiscovery software and other tools. With productization, the scaling opportunities for small and mid-sized legal practices is effectively infinite.

Another Reason to Productize Legal Services: The Public Interest

Wealthy people will always have access to top lawyers. But what about the rest of us non-rich[4] people who don't have the means to pay a legal bill that could, in just a few dozen billable hours, equate to the annual salary of the average working family? How do we defend ourselves from an eviction if we have no funds for rent, let alone a lawyer? How can we fight for child custody, or prove gender discrimination, or address any of the everyday wrongs people suffer if we can't afford legal representation—especially if facing an opponent with very deep pockets?

This gap in services—the "access to justice gap"—is gigantic. In the United States, one recent report[5] took a snapshot of a single year and found that:

---

4. I use the term "non-rich" intentionally. There are plenty of reasonably comfortable "middle class" people who simply can't afford the various professional services that might make their lives better. Hiring a lawyer, accountant, or the like is the bastion of rich people, and not always feasible for people of more limited means.

5. https://www.lsc.gov/media-center/publications/2017-justice-gap-report.

- 86 percent of the civil legal problems reported by low-income Americans received inadequate or no legal help.
- 71 percent of low-income households experienced at least one civil legal problem in the last year, including problems with health care, housing conditions, disability access, veterans' benefits, and domestic violence.
- Low-income Americans approached federally funded legal aid organizations for support with an estimated 1.7 million problems. They received only limited or no legal help for more than half of these problems due to a lack of resources.

The problem extends beyond those without the means to pay. There is also a "latent legal market" among the middle class. This term refers to the millions of people who have an actionable or justiciable issue that could be addressed through the legal system but who choose not to pursue it.[6] Recent American Bar Foundation research indicates that for every person who turns to the justice system for a legal matter, more than six do not. In many instances, this is because the would-be client doesn't have a legal service provider who can affordably meet their needs.

The pressure of all of these situations is quietly moving the legal industry from a purely service-oriented field to one that includes products that make the work of lawyering more efficient or that help clients navigate legal issues more effectively — sometimes, using an app or other tool without the need for a human lawyer.

Consider LegalZoom: This company has served a small slice of the "latent" market by making certain legal services — wills, contracts, incorporation papers — available to them through its website. The LegalZoom system guides the user through creating the document, and it does so in a workmanlike fashion, at a fraction the cost of a human counterpart. By doing so, LegalZoom has helped millions of people and achieved a valuation of several billion dollars to boot. They have done so by productizing legal services. But the frontier

---

6. For more, see this interview with Will Hornsby, of the American Bar Association, available at https://www.americanbar.org/groups/legal_services/publications/dialogue/volume/21/winter-2018/lris-guest-qa/.

remains open: Their work covers only a small fraction of the legal work that could be productized.

In the seminal work, *Tomorrow's Lawyers*, Richard Susskind argued that new methods and technologies have, and will continue, to emerge that allow many legal tasks to be done much more efficiently while leading both to better results for consumers of legal services and to profits for their creators. Law, or parts of it at least, are capable of being "commoditized" and made accessible to many more people, and at a lower cost. Susskind envisioned wholesale changes to the legal ecosystem. Some of these changes are already beginning to occur and can be seen in the growth of legal process outsourcing, eDiscovery tools, and other software that replaces legal associates' billable hours with computer programs.

In only the past few years, we have seen the rise of software solutions that directly compete with lawyers:

- Volunteers at CALI's A2J Author have automated thousands of forms that laypeople once struggled to complete on their own.
- Expert systems have helped capture decades of hard-earned knowledge about legal topics including immigration law, divorce law, and contract law into a single app.
- Law firms have created incubators—which function as in-house research and development labs—to build, test, and market new products and tools to sell to other lawyers and to consumers.
- Billions in funding have gone to support new startups in the market that are working to bring new efficiency to the legal industry. In some instances, this funding has created new tools that help law firms work more efficiently; others provide consumers with new, lower-cost forms of legal help; and in still others, these tools offer the underserved public free help that they might never have received otherwise.

Lawyers or law firms interested in productizing their service have a huge opportunity to make a difference. We can create tools that will help the poor when no lawyer is available to them. We can make tools that help middle-income people make the decision to get expert support when historically they would not have done so. Indeed, we can even make tools to embed within high-end companies' and firms' broad array of service offerings by making their repeatable work more efficient.

DO I NEED TO BE A COMPUTER PROGRAMMER TO PRODUCTIZE A SERVICE?

Let me say it up front: You do not need to know how to code to succeed at productizing legal services. I'm going to write it again, because it needs repeating: YOU DO NOT NEED TO KNOW HOW TO CODE TO DO THIS. It wouldn't hurt, the same way that it wouldn't hurt to have a pilot's license to become the CEO of an airline, but it's not necessary.

While some of the projects discussed in this book will involve some sophisticated understanding of technology, productization doesn't inherently require individuals working through the process to have coding skills. This is for two reasons: First, some forms of productization are done without writing a single line of code. Newsletters, seminars, and manuals, for example, are still very relevant and valuable—despite being very much *analog*. Second, even if your project does require coding, the preliminary work of discovering a project, building a prototype, and testing it out can be done using a new generation of tools that are made for non-techies. At the end of the book's process, readers will have a good idea if it makes sense to invest in an outside team to do the development work (and will have the ammunition needed to seek funding, too).

As we will discuss in more detail in chapter 3, productized services can take many forms: examples include an app, a website, software, or a tech tool such as a document assembly tool that makes filling out forms much more efficient. But a productized service isn't necessarily a tech tool. For example, turning a complicated process, like filing a patent application, into a series of easy-to-follow checklists is a productized service. Nor is there necessarily a profit motive behind every productized service. For example, volunteers at CALI's A2J Author created guided online interviews that automated thousands of forms laypeople once struggled to complete on their own. There are all kinds of productized services.

WHAT IS THE PROCESS OF PRODUCTIZING A SERVICE?

Productizing a service is a *process*. It is the process of identifying a legal service that has traditionally been done (typically by a lawyer or a paralegal) for individual end users (a client, for example) and developing it into a *product* that can provide that same legal service more quickly, more easily, and to many more end users. This book provides a foundational understanding of this very useful and valuable process, and this chapter offers an overview of the different steps or stages of that process.

This book lays out a process for identifying problems that can be solved by productizing a service, validating your theories about solving them, and making a plan to bring them to the world as productized services. Throughout the book are activities that will allow you to take this process on, step by step.

The challenge of mapping out a process for productizing a service is that it isn't always consistently linear. Sometimes, on the basis of new information, it is wise to loop back and repeat an earlier step. At other times, there may be sound reasons for going out of order. With that caveat in mind, here is a brief explanation of each step in the process of developing a productized service. The chapters that follow provide a fuller discussion of each, as well as case studies, real-life stories from experts in the field, examples, and exercises meant to convey a working knowledge of the core concepts and real-world skills of productization and to deepen your understanding of each stage.

Step One: Identify the Problem or Need that Productizing Could Solve

Before going through the time, effort, and expense of building a productized service, it's important to have evidence that the product will solve a problem that people need solved. This means "starting at the end" by defining a problem that can be solved with a productized service and identifying an end user that would benefit from it.

Step Two: Survey the Competitive Environment

New products that replicate existing ones will fail, unless there's a good reason for customers to switch over. The way to identify competition is to do some basic research. Develop a sense of what is out there, including both direct competitors (those solving the same problem in a similar way) and indirect competitors (those solving the same problem using a different method). For example, a law firm that does patent searches would be an indirect competitor to an app that searches for patents.

Step Three: Elevator Pitch

A terrific technique for gauging response from potential users of a productized service is to boil your idea down to an "elevator pitch." This is a short, persuasive speech you use to introduce yourself (if necessary) and tell someone about your idea. Its purpose is to explain the concept quickly and clearly to spark interest in who you are and what you do.

Step Four: Build a Prototype

Creating a model of the productized service—a prototype—serves several functions. It helps to hone the idea, it will be necessary to use when demonstrating the concept to others, and it lends legitimacy and seriousness to the project. Plus, it can be fun!

Step Five: Seek Feedback from End Users

Interviewing end users (the people the product

A key part of developing new ideas is to build prototypes and to test them with both experts and end users. In fact, when you read on, you'll encounter an entire chapter on the art of building prototypes and another on soliciting and implementing feedback on them. Well, this book is itself a form of productizing of my own services. Because of that, I'd be a hypocrite if, in making it, I didn't follow the same creation process I propose to you. So that's exactly what I did. I designed around end users. I asked experts. I reached out to people I envision as end users of the book. I created prototypes in the form of drafts of every chapter you will read and sought feedback from lots of people. I asked people to step up and share their views. I listened to the advice and feedback, and I took it seriously. In writing this book, I did what I'll ask you to do: I iterated on the prototype, and I made the subsequent versions better.

is designed for) helps to identify what they like about the concept and the prototype that demonstrates it, as well as what they want more of and whether they would pay for, or adopt, the product.

Step Six: Build a Business Case

For most projects, getting external support—whether in the form of money or time away from typical duties—is necessary to get things off the ground. Even for those who don't need external support, creating a business case by creating a "pitch deck" (a common tool for those seeking funding) helps to identify challenges and consider ways to resolve them.

Step Seven: Special Issues for Lawyers and Legal Product Makers

Because law is a regulated industry, creating products to address legal problems can trigger a number of issues that must be considered, from avoiding allegations that one is engaged in the "unauthorized practice of law" to the need for attorneys to consider whether a productized service is covered under their malpractice policy.

Step Eight: Planning for Launch

Before a productized service goes public, taking pre-operation steps to market it using mailing lists, talks at CLE events, and more, will help to get traction for the project even before it launches.

Step Nine: Launch (and Beyond)

From the moment of launch onward, a series of new opportunities and challenges arise. This step gives guidance on launch day marketing, how to handle weaker-than-expected results, and how to handle success.

WHY LEARN HOW TO PRODUCTIZE LEGAL WORK?

Regardless of your interest in product innovation, understanding the development process is valuable. It will expand your awareness of developments in your field. It will help you better identify the needs of your clients. It may even help to future-proof your career in law, as new technologies emerge that might render certain traditional legal services obsolete.

Not every effort to make a productized service will be a smashing success (though we will work to maximize your chances!). Even if a product does not change the industry, the process of making it requires the sort of introspection, research, and discussion that we should all strive to employ to better understand our work and our clients' needs, regardless of what we aim to get out of it.

This book introduces you to a process for creating something that will allow you to be more efficient, to serve more end users, or to do better work for clients at a lower cost to them. If you work for profit, it has to potentially increase your bottom line. If you work in the public or nonprofit sector, it can help you give more people access to expertise without having to hire additional staff members to provide it.

Exercise: The Growth of Productization

What productized services have you encountered in your own life, within the law and outside of it? As an end user of these products, how did using them benefit you? How did the experience differ from the experience you expect you might have had if you had used the traditional service that the product replaced?

Reflection Question

You have experienced tools in your everyday life that use technology to replace repetitive human work—for example, when you encounter an automated toll booth on the highway, or when you call your local utility company and receive automated customer support. What are the benefits and drawbacks of these automated services for you, the end user? What do you think are the benefits and drawbacks of these tools for the organizations that implemented them?

Chapter 2

Unbundling Legal Work

T raditionally, a client expected their attorney to handle every aspect of their case. A divorce lawyer, for example, would interview the client to identify their needs, perform legal research on their behalf, write correspondence, draft and file the relevant court filings, calculate the financial documents required for dividing assets, take depositions, hire expert witnesses, create trial exhibits, and conduct the trial itself (and much more). Then, around the year 2000, came unbundling: This is an approach to legal services that takes all of the discrete things an attorney does and asks if each of those tasks is being done in the most efficient way. If not, rather than the attorney doing the work, technology (for example, electronic discovery software) replaces the lawyer or paralegal who had been reading thousands of pages of documents. The traditional lawyer or paralegal's role on a given task was replaced by more cost-effective technology or a niche expert (for example, an accountant trained in legal matters to create the financial reports needed in a divorce case).

Once the work of representing a client is mapped out (depending on the situation, this could be done by the attorney, an in-house counsel representing the client, or a combination of the two), identifying step by step the many tasks required in that representation, the work of unbundling can begin by determining the most efficient means of accomplishing each discrete task. One of those common paths—and hence from our perspective one of the opportunities— is through productized services. Thus, if an attorney historically drafted an Answer to a Complaint as part of defending a lawsuit, taking three hours to do so, a productized service in the form of an app that can quickly scan the Complaint and generate an Answer using machine learning would be a useful unbundling tool. For those who are entrepreneurial and have a good understanding of both an area of law practice and of the capabilities of various technologies, it is possible to identify opportunities to build niche productized services that fit into unbundled legal work.

When done correctly, unbundling leaves the attorney with less grunt work and significantly more time to focus on what they do best: exercising creativity, judgment, and empathy, and thinking strategically about their client's case. In this way, unbundling can combine the best of legal representation and productization of legal services by directing the attorney's scope of involvement to those tasks for which an attorney is indispensable.

In the unbundled model of legal practice, the lawyer is like a quarterback, providing a game plan for the client and direction to service companies playing a specialized role in the game (one company might summarize medical records, for example, and another might perform electronic discovery). Unbundling maximizes the number of clients an attorney or law office can serve, while minimizing the number of billable hours their clients must pay. Through the practice of unbundling, clients can have access to a lawyer when they need one and use unbundled legal services for everything else.

UNBUNDLING BRINGS CHALLENGES TO LEGAL PROFESSIONALS AND THE LEGAL PROFESSION AS A WHOLE

Entire companies specializing in unbundling, alternative legal service providers (ALSP), have entered the marketplace to take advantage of these opportunities. Essentially, these providers are willing to be general contractors for legal work, figuring out who can fulfill a task forming part of a legal matter most effectively (whether it is the ALSP itself that does the work, or contracts it out) and at the best price.

The range of unbundled legal services regularly covered by alternative legal service providers is broad. it might include some or all of the following, and more:

- Advising clients of rights, appropriate legal actions, and likely outcomes;
- Drafting documents (petitions, motions, declarations, responses, replies, proposed orders, settlement offers, etc.);

- Reviewing documents drafted by clients;
- Reviewing proposals sent by the client's opponent;
- Filing court documents;
- Negotiating with the other party;
- Preparing/coaching the client to self-represent in court.[1]

Their impact has been profound: In a study by Thomson Reuters's Legal Executive Institute, the majority of firms surveyed, including small firms, used an ALSP to handle at least one category of work they had traditionally done themselves.[2] Among large law firms, 87 percent did so. They are not just getting small bits of work, either: The ALSP industry generated over $10 billion in a single year.

This will have real, and increasing, impact on legacy law firms. Two major categories of ALSP will be difficult for traditional law firms to compete with. The first relies on offshoring work at lower cost to places with lower costs of living. The second category is made of better-known companies: The Big Four accounting firms have expanded into the legal services market. These firms are capable of doing everything from taking on traditional legal work (like drafting agreements or performing research), to management consulting aimed specifically at the legal sector. These huge firms have long focused on promoting efficiency in other sectors, and they are able to apply lessons learned in accounting and elsewhere to law.

The Big Four are in the process of rebranding themselves: No longer "alternatives," they want to be recognized as "new law" or "law companies."[3] What will this mean for the future of legal practice?

On the plus side, it will mean that law firms and corporations will be using the services of trusted, US-based vendors that can provide services more efficiently than a big law firm could.

On the other hand, these "law companies" will not only take work away from existing law firms and legal providers, they will also change the very nature of the relationship between attorney and client. When an attorney is directly responsible for all aspects of a

---

1. https://www.northwestadvocacy.org/resourceposts/2019/4/25/unbundled.

2. https://www.legalexecutiveinstitute.com/alsp-report-2019/.

3. https://www.law.com/legaltechnews/2020/02/14/alsp-new-law-or-law-company -whats-behind-legals-shifting-identity/.

client's matter, that attorney is forced to master every piece of it, to think deeply about the case, and to dedicate time to the situation. Contrast this with the attorney who relies on the unbundled services of a "law company." In this scenario, the attorney of record (at the law firm) is responsible for collecting and patching together the many pieces of work done by others (in the "law company"). While each piece may have been done quite competently, the attorney managing the matter no longer exercises the same high level of involvement in every aspect of the case that one might hope for from one's attorney—a qualitative loss to the client. This model of unbundling can also be good for clients, however, because it saves them money on legal representation.

Lawyers who are unwilling to engage in an unbundled approach, who represent clients exclusively on a "full service" basis, will find themselves increasingly unable to compete with the cost efficiencies of ALSPs. Take the stereotypical small town general practitioner: They make a decent living by treating people well and solving the legal problems they present. On one day the client may need a will drafted, on another clients may need to sue a contractor that did a poor job fixing their roof, and on a third, they may present a contract to be reviewed. In this situation, the attorney gets to know their client's needs and desires, the way a long-time primary care doctor anticipates their patients' needs. If this work is unbundled, however, the client might get lower cost representation on any

Similar shifts are happening in the broader world of knowledge work. For example, traditional strategy consulting firms now offer unbundled services—work done for clients who hire them *a la carte* to solve more focused problems. Consequently, the share of traditional strategy work done at consulting companies has decreased from 60 or 70 percent in the 1980s[4] to 20 percent today. McKinsey Solutions, for example, offers software and technology-based analytics that do much of the work that a human consultant would have shared with clients, except the information is updated in real time and clients can access it whenever needed.

---

4. https://hbr.org/2013/10/consulting-on-the-cusp-of-disruption.

of the matters using productized services. The clients' savings are the attorney's loss because, in this situation, the two are in direct conflict. ALSPs can take advantage of labor cost arbitrage to save unbundled law firms money, which makes some tasks that full-service lawyers have traditionally performed no longer economically feasible. Simply put, a successful litigator in a major US city simply can't compete, in terms of cost (and increasingly, on quality), with a specialist eDiscovery expert who lives in the developing world and can use the legal skills gained in her own law degree (earned in her own country) for a fraction of the cost.

UNBUNDLING BRINGS NEW OPPORTUNITIES TO LEGAL PROFESSIONALS, TOO

Despite concerns that unbundling will change legal work for the worse, it offers tantalizing opportunities for legal professionals as well. First, it opens up entirely new areas for helping clients. Some clients will hire a law firm to handle only certain aspects of a case. Still others will hire a law firm at a certain price point, and unbundling could make what was otherwise unfeasible for the client affordable.

Second, there is no way to meet the legal needs of lower-income people using the traditional billable hour model. Using unbundled services, particularly in forms like document automation systems that allow people to self-help in filling out some legal forms, can significantly reduce the immense gap in providing full access to legal services.

Finally, to take legal work seriously means to put the needs of clients first. Clients should have maximum control over their legal matters, in terms of controlling

Just a few years after the iPhone was invented, investor Marc Andreeson wrote an op-ed in the *Wall Street Journal* arguing that "software is eating the world."[5] At that time, it was only brainy MIT-types who were gorging, though. Being a software developer took deep skills gained over a lifetime of learning. Now, however, "low code" and "no code" tools

---

5. https://www.wsj.com/articles/SB10001424053111903480904576512250915629460.

both how the work is done and how much it will cost. This is the fiduciary duty that all attorneys owe their clients, and part and parcel of that is assuring that clients receive the appropriate legal services at a fair cost.

allow amateurs to create their own sophisticated software with just a few minutes of training. These tools are to sophisticated software development what Pillsbury Crescent Rolls are to the art of making pastry: You can just pop it out of the container and put it on a backing sheet, and it's pretty darn good. No French cooking school training required.

Reflection Question

Consider some knowledge-based services that either you provided for others (for example, advising a client), or that you yourself used (tax preparation, medical care, retirement planning). Consider the various tasks that are integral to any one of these services. For each task that you can think of, ask yourself: Is there a lower-cost way to accomplish the same task than having it performed by a professional?

Chapter 3

Patterns of Productization

This chapter describes many of the categories of productized service that have already been created, illustrating their range for those interested in creating a new one themselves. Productized services come in all shapes, sizes, and scopes. Some amount to an entire business that fully replaces the work of a human. Others are tools enabling end users to remove some small piece of human intervention in the work they do to meet a client's needs. In fact, it is wise to think of productization as a portfolio: Try many ideas, test products in different areas and with different target markets, and diversify your offerings to spread your risk across a range of offerings.[1] Nonetheless, every bundle of services must begin with

In 1975, the experimental musician and producer Brian Eno created the game Oblique Strategies, consisting of a set of cards. The size of playing cards, Eno's cards each offered a challenging constraint intended to help artists break creative blocks and encourage lateral thinking. When a musician couldn't decide what to do in the studio, Eno would ask them to pick a card, read and reflect on it, and use that as their starting point. Aptly called "oblique," the cards were intended to give a broad foundation, rather than being overly specific; examples include "use an old idea" and "work at a different speed." The challenge of being unable to start when one lacks a clear mission is what psychologists call the "blank canvas"

---

1. For more on this, see Dennis Kennedy's essay on productization which, for me, was foundational to my interest in this area: https://www.denniskennedy.com/blog/2019/04/productization-of-legal-services-2014-version/.

a single one, and the following are just some of the many examples of successful products already created.

Productized services can also serve different functions for those who create them. Some will primarily be an additional source of revenue. Others will not directly lead to revenue but can help promote the creator of the content. Still other information products problem: Having no guideposts for what to do can be frustrating and lead to hesitation because there are simply too many options to easily choose one.

You, too, might face the blank canvas problem as you start. You want to make something valuable, but *what*? There's so much to accomplish in the productization of legal services—how can you choose just one? Channeling Eno and Oblique Strategies, those facing blank canvases can benefit from taking on some constraints. This list of categories of productized services can help provide one.

will serve primarily as a pro bono opportunity to help others to get training or information who might not otherwise be able to afford it. And, of course, the productized service you create can serve as any combination of the above.

EXPERT INSIGHT FROM JARED CORREIA

Moving toward law firm products makes sense for both the lawyer and the client. For the client, law products fall more in line with the way that they purchase goods across the modern economy. When a consumer can purchase the century-old streaming library of a multimedia conglomerate for less than $100/year, a lawyer asking for a $5,000 retainer for some amorphous project with dubious value probably comes off like a Martian. Legal products, if constructed correctly, can provide modern legal consumers what they want: a fixed price, and a clear value proposition.

* * *

Jared D. Correia, Esq., is a business management consultant for lawyers and has developed a chatbot service built for lawyers. He can be reached at jared@redcavelegal.com.

Not just any work can be converted into a service: It makes sense in only a certain subset. As a general observation, the most successful productized services are tasks that do not rely on judgment. They can be complex, but they cannot require implicit decision-making. For example, preparing a personal income tax return in the United States is the bane of millions trying to decide which figure is divided by which other figure; equally challenging is deciding what line to put the answer on. However, there's not much judgment baked in. Simply put, a taxpayer either does or does not have a home with a mortgage and, from there, it's a simple calculation to determine what deduction that mortgage allows. Contrast that with the role of the web designer charged with creating a website that will fit the mood of a fancy gala. Certainly some generally applicable design principles provide guidelines, but a ton of issues requiring subjective judgment remain. We can productize a template to capture the basics, but as a stand-alone project, it will either require a designer's finishing touch or a customer for whom "good enough" is good enough.

Finally, while it is typically best to start off slow (e.g., try a single, one-hour webinar before launching a 10-hour online course), having a sense of the possible can, and will, lead to a more productive choice on where to start.[2] The work of innovation requires pushing the envelope, so if you've got an idea that doesn't fall into the categories here, don't consider it a bad one. It simply means you'll be sailing in uncharted territories (or, at the very least, territories I haven't seen charted in law).

---

2. Because the most interesting examples and resources across these topics change over time, please see the online appendix for up-to-date information.

QUICK KEY TO TYPES OF PRODUCTIZED SERVICES

Information Products

- eBooks
- webinars
- online courses
- newsletters
- checklists
- manuals

Decision Support and Document Automation

- expert system
- document automation
- triage and referral

Calculators

Data

INFORMATION PRODUCTS

Information products take information, intellectual property, and know-how that's useful to others and package it into something that's easily shared at scale. It's a way to educate clients or train others in an expertise that you have attained in a subspecialty so that they can do likewise.

Two categories not mentioned below are podcasts and blogs. Both are, at least arguably, productized services to the extent they take content one might deliver to a small group (like emails or talks a consultant would provide to a group on the state of innovation in their industry). For the most part, however, podcasts and blogs operate in a unique space between journalism and opinion. Dozens of excellent resources already out there guide people looking to create blogs and podcasts (There are even blogs on creating blogs and podcasts on creating podcasts!) so, on balance, it seemed unnecessary to include them here.

eBook

eBooks are short books (often as brief as 10,000 words) written on a focused topic and published digitally. Often, eBooks are made available at low or no cost and are used to both convey knowledge to readers and to help promote the author as a "thought leader." Very few people get rich by writing an eBook,[3] but the effort can improve your profile and indirectly lead to other opportunities. Plus, it's cool to say you wrote a book, and an eBook counts (if anyone says it doesn't, show them this page for confirmation).

eBooks are excellent tools both to spread ideas in bite-sized formats and to earn extra money. They can be sold through several channels, from purpose-made book selling platforms (like Amazon) to websites that specialize in eBook creation to your own website.

They're also straightforward to create: An eBook that will be offered in an online store can be created using several free and low-cost tools to format it to be read on Kindles or other eReaders. If the eBook will be offered at no cost—as a means of promoting a person or business—it can simply be formatted using a free book template and converted into a PDF. Then, when a person wants to read it, they enter their email address on a website, and the file is automatically mailed to the reader: This is easy, efficient, and allows the content-creator to track leads on who is reading their work and might be interested in the problems the eBook solves.

In terms of content, consider doing a deep dive on a very narrow subject. Examples are an eBook on handling sidebar conversations at trial or on creating trust provisions to handle descendants' upkeep expenses on a vacation house. The goal here is to attract a niche audience and address their specific need.

Webinar

A webinar is a relatively short—normally an hour or less—video that is aired live. It's a useful tool to teach someone a skill or

---

3. With plenty of notable exceptions. Self-improvement/entrepreneurship wiz Tim Ferriss has blogged on this topic and highlighted several people who make a generous full-time living self-publishing eBooks, https://tim.blog/2013/04/04/how-to-make-1000000-selling-e-books-tactics-and-case-studies/.

a discrete area of knowledge, and it offers an easy way to advertise your expertise and attract people to bigger products, like membership sites and courses. In some ways, you can think of this as giving a CLE talk on something you know a lot about—except, in the form of a webinar, you can scale it much larger.

Creating a webinar isn't too time-consuming. Preparing a basic webinar requires only a detailed outline of the content. Equipment needs are light too: a laptop with a video camera and some basic understanding of how to use video conference software (like how to identify questions and respond to them, as well as how to deal with glitches that come up). There are several easy-to-use, low-cost tools that make this feasible for people with modest tech skills.

Controlling and selling access is relatively easy, too. If you intend to have a paywall, you can use a special webinar hosting platform. Alternately, you can do something as simple as creating a Zoom or GoToMeeting link and then sharing it with people who indicate an interest in attending. Zoom now even includes webinar integration in its standard offering, so you can easily incorporate payment.

Online Course

If you graduated from school many years ago, you may have never experienced an online course. In short, they're changing the way people learn and creating new opportunities for experts to teach an audience vastly larger than they could ever reach in a physical lecture hall. Just like traditional classes, online classes teach students how to understand or do something across several sessions.

Creating a good course from scratch is a challenge, even for professional educators. To do it right will require a willingness to learn about course design and to plot out the content. Typically, you can expect to put in at least ten hours of work for every one hour of content created. However, once created, content can be "evergreen" and result in passive income for a long time.

Several platforms make creating and marketing online courses feasible. At a minimum, it will require a computer and software to capture video/screen. Some people have run successful online courses with little more than a set of PowerPoints and their recorded voices running over them to narrate the slides. More professional content can be much more involved, but coordinating all the things necessary beyond filming the video (marketing, sales, getting CLE credit eligibility, setting up payment systems) is the real challenge.

There are several options for hosting, though. Creators can use a hosting platform and their eCommerce system but do the promotion themselves. Alternatively, creators can use platforms that do the promotion; this will result in a bigger audience reached, but a lower margin and less control for creators. Finally, creators can create a password protected area on their website and sell access via an eCommerce platform.

This is a "big" play, but also one with potentially big benefits. Consider financial expert, Ramit Sethi, who has created an empire around productizing his advice through books and online courses. He claims to have made over $600,000 on his first class alone.[4]

Case Study: Suffolk Law Legal Innovation and Technology Certificate Program

When I speak to bar associations and at conferences for legal professionals about the legal tech program at Suffolk Law, the single most common question from the audience is "How can I learn those things?" The truth is, it's hard to learn how to automate, process map, engage in design thinking, and identify business options in "new law" on your own. Almost everything that exists in the legal realm is aimed at JDs (and there's not enough of that!). CLE sessions and events can help open the audience's eyes, but they are too short to help people learn substantive skills (especially when they are working a full-time job).

After several years of thinking about how we might help solve this problem for legal professionals (and not just attorneys either—there's a screaming need for legal tech education for paralegals, librarians, and others), I worked with colleagues at Suffolk Law to launch an online program for legal professionals to meet this need. The program

---

4. https://growthlab.com/how-do-i-create-and-sell-online-courses/.

(www.legaltechcertificate.com) launched in 2018 and consists of six fully online courses, each with about 10 hours of video lectures, combined with reading to be done outside of the sessions, assignments, and message boards. It's taught by the people we think are, quite literally, the best in the world in the given areas.

It took a lot of work to get it off the ground: The easy part was recruiting instructors. From there, we had to work with them to design a syllabus, adapt their teaching to an online format, and create assignments and message board prompts. We worked with a team of instructional designers to get this done. We also involved marketers, sales experts, and IT people to make sure the infrastructure was in place to make it all work and to let people know about the content. There were some added regulatory hurdles because it's being offered by a law school, and still other hurdles to get CLE credit.

We've been rewarded for this work—within a year of starting the program, we had students from every inhabited continent on earth—and the program is bearing fruit for those who have participated. Having said that, it's still lots of work on our end: making sure the students are learning, the instructors are happy, and the details are handled requires daily effort. As a nonprofit, we don't focus on profitability, but we need to manage revenue and expenses, too, which can be a challenge.

Newsletter

In the Internet era, a newsletter is a regularly updated message that comes to subscribers by email to give them updates or curated information about a topic of specific interest to them. Plenty of big players—from the *New York Times* to CNN—have a daily newsletter, but the best opportunity in the area of productization is to use newsletters to update readers on a niche topic with specific appeal (e.g., updates for the med-mal defense bar in Delaware, or reviews of new eDiscovery software). There are several free tools for creating, formatting, and delivering newsletters. They are often free to use up to 1,000 or more subscribers. Making them is simple, too: You just need a computer to use the software, and it is helpful to have knowledge about social media to promote the newsletter. Finally, a number of channels offer means to grow a subscriber base for your newsletter.

Companies are emerging that promote newsletters (and take a cut of subscription prices in exchange), while others share them for free as a way to promote their firm or business. Popular newsletters also earn money on ad revenue. A newsletter, however, can be as simple an undertaking as emailing it to subscribers via the free software.

Case Study: Lawtomatic Newsletter

More than two years before I started writing this book, I launched a weekly newsletter—the Lawtomatic Newsletter—focused on products and productization in legal services. I kept it up too. It was only after writing the one-hundredth weekly edition that I declared that I was going on sabbatical (to write this book). It has been my only hiatus during the academic year in the time since I started it.

I started the newsletter because I was already informally sending a number of articles around every week to students and colleagues I thought might be interested. Simple stuff: a link with a sentence or so as to why it was relevant to legal tech products. After several months doing this without much thought, it occurred to me that for little more effort, I could reach many more people than just sending a weekly email around.

I used the same concept as I had for my email but remade into a newsletter: a weekly message with five things worth reading every week, each with a sentence or so of commentary. I chose five because it seemed right, and also because I subscribe to efficiency guru Tim Ferriss's free newsletter, Five Bullet Friday, which also includes five items.

I signed up for a TinyLetter account—which was free—and posted a link to Twitter and LinkedIn encouraging people who liked it to give me their email address so I could deliver it to them directly. My subscriber list quickly grew past 1,000 followers, and once all the LinkedIn shares and retweets are done, the link goes to tens of thousands every week.

This has been a terrific way to spread ideas I think are important, make new connections, and build and maintain a network. The newsletter has had several sponsors.

(Sponsors provide a link and line of text on what they want to promote. I identify it for readers as a paid ad, and readers can click or skip past the link as they see fit.) I've made money on the project, too. Not "vacation house" money, but certainly "pay for the family vacation" money. It has also led to some fun moments, like someone reading my nametag at the big, annual conference for law librarians and exclaiming (with more excitement than it deserved, perhaps): "Oh wow, the Lawtomatic Newsletter guy!" It's been a nice way to connect with new people and a nice way to remind people I know that I still exist in the world and have ideas to share. It remains a resource for my students and colleagues, just like the email I used to send them.

There are some downsides: Some weeks I don't feel like putting in the time to gather the links or to write a succinct statement as to why anyone should care about it. Also, as the audience has grown, I've felt more of a need to carefully edit it, which takes a bit of fun out of the process. I've controlled expectations in a few ways, including letting readers know I would only publish during the academic year, and striking a fairly colloquial tone so that a stray typo doesn't seem to stop the music. A goal I have for the future is to get better at segmenting subscribers: People who approach me about sponsoring the newsletter want to know who will be seeing it. My current newsletter tool just tracks people by name and email. A better system would allow newsletter creators to gather other information: geographic location, job title, years in the field, etc.

Checklist

Not all productized legal services require a computer science degree or the cash to hire a development team. Take checklists, for example. These are a prime productization opportunity for experienced professionals who have created a system to promote efficiency, organize their work, and reduce errors: Checklists memorialize their process. Some of these will be devoted to the business of law (like checklists for starting up a new firm); others may focus on best practices for attorneys (e.g., a checklist for documents to request when investigating nursing home litigation matters); still others might be aimed at the pro se litigant (e.g., a checklist of evidence a tenant should bring to court when facing an eviction matter).

Checklists require nothing more than a computer to write them out and a printer to print them. However, checklists also make sense as content to embed in a subscription website or app. For example, attorney Julie Savarino (featured in chapter 4) created a checklist approach for her law firm clients to help them prepare for pitching clients. She subsequently embedded those checklists in an app, and later included them in a book.

The sales channel may dictate how the checklists are shared. For example, professional organizations that sell continuing education materials may be open to promoting specialized checklists. They can also be sold through a personal website or shared at no added cost in combination with a webinar or other training. Finally, it is common for checklist creators to share them freely (or, at the least, for goodwill/marketing benefit) among their bar organization or circle of professional contacts.

Manual

If you've ever been tasked with onboarding a secretary or training a new paralegal to join your established firm, you've likely either used a manual created internally or wished you had one. If you've created a good one, you'll be doing a service by making it a product offered to others. In its essence, a manual is a memorialization of the processes for how a given organization operates, both in general and with respect to a specific set of tasks. It will often include supplemental sample materials (like letters and forms). The manual effectively stands in for the live supervisor in guiding aspects of an underling's training or daily work. In many instances, the manual will be created for internal purposes, and the information might just need polishing to be of value to others. This means that making a manual into something useful to others will require little more than some editing and formatting.

Much like with checklists, continuing education organizations may be open to selling manuals, though they can also be sold directly through personal websites or given as course materials for a corresponding online course/webinar that teaches how to use the manual. In this case, contributing a chapter—with attribution to you and/or your firm—can pay dividends in indirect opportunities, like improving your reputation and making you more likely to get referrals as a result.

Manuals can also be used to help legal professionals become more adept as business operators. For example, in 1983, Canadian legal marketing expert Patrick McKenna founded the company now known as Edge International.

EXPERT INSIGHT FROM PATRICK MCKENNA

I developed the first TV advertising (high-class, 1-minute info-mercials) and packaged a product composed of scripts, print and yellow pages advertising and signed on 5 major law firms across 2 Provinces, each in a different geographical location. The informational scripts covered all kind of legal issues from simple estate planning and personal injury (individual consumer) to litigation prevention and entrepreneurial issues. The advertising worked!

Lawyers had no idea what to do when the phones rang. Rather than arranging for the prospect to come in for an appointment, they dispensed free legal advice over the telephone; they did not know how to actively listen; how to ask for a retainer; how to manage the client's expectations; how to cross-sell or any number of other skills (not knowledge) issues—which allowed for the development of a number of different training modules. These modules were developed with separate participant workbooks, a facilitators' manual and an accompanying 8-minute video presentation (with each) showing a real lawyer with their client performing the skill and then breaking it down to some simple steps to follow. It was a program designed as an example of learn by doing, rather than thinking that some lawyer would effectively learn from being lectured to or by reading an article/book.

*   *   *

Patrick McKenna is an an author, lecturer, strategist, and seasoned advisor to the leaders of premier firms. He can be reached at patrick.mckenna@attglobal.net.

DECISION SUPPORT AND DOCUMENT AUTOMATION

One of the greatest values of the Internet for society has been that it changes our relationship with knowledge. The answers to vexing questions are available to anyone with access to the web in ways that they never have been before.

For knowledge professionals, the web has a remarkable potential as a platform to help clients reach answers to hard questions, and, in some instances, to harness technology to create the forms and other documents needed. These two concepts—of decision support and document assembly—are often packaged into a single product. For example, tax software uses detailed knowledge of the federal income tax system to ask users questions (Are you married? Do you have a mortgage?) and then, as appropriate, takes the user's answers and calculates and fills in the corresponding line of the tax return. Ultimately, the software asks the user all the right questions, and the user gets a tax return to file.

Expert System

Imagine having a robot assistant interact with you in a given context like a knowledgeable person would. For example, if you need to do your taxes, the robot would ask you if you were married to learn if you should consider filing jointly; based on your answer, it would ask follow-up questions to help advise you on its analysis. This is how popular consumer tax software companies operate, and it's an increasingly accessible technology for professionals willing to think through their work, step by step, and consider all the different paths their advice might take, given different facts.

In short, an expert system is a software tool that uses decision tree logic representing the questions an expert would ask on a given topic to help end users guide decisions and offer advice. It simulates an expert with knowledge in an area that can be parsed into binary, yes/no, or multiple-option knowledge with no gray areas. The value of expert systems is that when there is a complex decision to be made, the system will ask the right question at the right moment. The challenge is that a lot of nested questions and subtle judgments are or can be implicit in decision-making, and creating an expert system requires practice in recognizing that and working around it appropriately.

Building an expert system today is not a difficult technological challenge, because so many companies have created excellent low-code and no-code tools. To make an expert system, the content creator simply needs a computer with inexpensive, sometimes free, software to develop it.

You'll also need a lot of time. The process of creating a decision tree—spelling out each potential path to solve a given legal problem—takes patience, experience, and, well, expertise. The good news is that ramping up is relatively easy, and preliminary steps can be done on sticky notes or using index cards. Once the expert system is done, keep in mind that in many instances you will have to make more changes in the future. If the law changes, a new option becomes available, or your own analysis of how best to handle the challenge changes, you'll have to go back and update the chart.

Once the system is created, there are all different ways to share it with others. It can be a stand-alone website, embedded in a firm or company's existing site, or turned into an app. Depending on the goals of the project, you might add a paywall to the site or instead think of it as a marketing tool. Beyond that, various expert systems products have been made available as a community resource or pro bono project. For those without access to professional legal advice, having a well-designed expert system encoded with a professional's knowledge can be a useful substitute to answer law-related questions and solve legal matters.

Document Automation

Document automation, also called document assembly, is a software tool to assist people in efficiently filling out or creating electronic documents. Sometimes, these systems use segments of preexisting text and/or data to assemble a new document. This process is increasingly used within certain industries to assemble legal documents, insurance forms, and frequently sent letters. Document automation systems can also be used to automate all conditional text (for example, in generating a will, if a person answers "yes" to a question about having children, the software could then ask follow-up questions about them), variable text (for example, in a criminal record expungement, the software could ask a different set of follow-up questions for those convicted of a felony than those convicted of only misdemeanors), and data contained within a set of documents (for example, in a divorce case, by making proposed alimony payments based on information about salary and assets contained in financial disclosures based on a formula used in the courts).

Document automation tools work best when there's a high volume of conditional logic required to fill out the form. Imagine a name change petition being filed in family court. If the person seeking to have their name changed is, or has been, married, the court will likely require information about their spouse. If not, they skip that section. In the context of a document assembly tool, the system might ask "Have you ever been married?" If the answer is yes, it will ask the user to fill in their spouse's information; if not, it will simply skip that section and move to the next (and a well-designed system might have a pop-up that explains *why* the system is asking that question). This is in contrast to a fillable online form, where the user fills in every blank and just clicks tabs between each one to advance. For the typical fillable form, no document automation tool is needed, because it won't save any time—or provide any guidance—because the user is filling out each blank in any event.

These tools have never been easier to use, with a generation of them being made as low-code or no-code. Even for those with no experience in making them, it's feasible to dig in and create one. In fact, I've taught classrooms of law students with no computer science or programming experience each of the last several years to use document assembly tools, and all have been able to successfully create something—often with no technical guidance.

Many of the software packages that are built for document assembly allow content creators to automate Word documents. Some commonly automated forms include:

- Contracts
- Contingent fee agreements
- Complaints and accompanying documents
- Discovery requests
- Freedom of Information Act request letters
- Insurance forms
- Medical record and bill requests
- Non-disclosure agreements

Many tools also allow creators to automate PDF files. These are often court forms or forms from government agencies, like:

- Small claims complaints
- Immigration Court notices of appearance
- Crash reports (following a car accident)
- Name change applications[5]

Document assembly systems also have an interface that allows people to create guided interviews to go along with the form, so that the user's process in filling out the document has a conversational tone. In this sense, document assembly systems overlap with expert systems by using branching logic to ask the next question. Doing this requires a workflow that moves users through the form, step by step, varying the order and coverage based on the individual user's needs.

Document assembly tools can be overlaid on other technologies, including email. For example, several years ago, I got fed up with receiving "late" Amazon Prime packages. At that time, the contract called for any package to be delivered within two days, and if Amazon failed to do so, the customer who paid for Prime would get a free month of the service unless a few limited exceptions applied. Using document assembly software, I wrote a program that asked the user to confirm that none of the narrow exceptions applied, then to type in their name, order number, and a few other key pieces of information. In turn, the tool generated an email to Amazon's customer service claiming the added month of service and providing the evidence for it. This generated a lot of extra Prime service for me and other users of the tool![6] Other projects have done similar conceptual work, including tools to generate Freedom of Information Act requests to government agencies or to notify a member of Congress about a constituent's feelings on pending legislation.

---

5. This is a very small sampling of document assembly projects that can be coupled with a guided interview. For a far wider range, look at LawHelpInteractive.org. This website collects document assembly projects intended to support the access to justice community. Projects on the site are made by volunteers who post them for use by others at no cost. Some are intended to be completed by pro se litigants; others help legal professionals more efficiently serve their clients.

6. Amazon ultimately changed its policies so that a late Prime order no longer merited a free month of service. I cannot claim to have been the ultimate cause of that, but there's another important lesson there: Document automation tools are only as effective as their accuracy based on the underlying law they're applied to. Once Amazon's rules changed, the tool became useless except as a teaching example.

The software to create these tools tends to be low-cost, or the company behind it offers a basic freemium version but unlocks additional features to users of the paid version. Some document assembly tools are both free and open-source, with a community of supporters improving them regularly.

Various platforms exist to sell your document assembly tool to others. Some companies have their own servers that host the guided interviews, while others are able to white label it so that it includes your branding and appears to be your own invention.

CONSIDERING A DOCUMENT ASSEMBLY PROJECT? START HERE

Excerpted from "Keys to a Successful Document Assembly Project," by Marc Lauritsen and Alan Soudakoff. Copyright © 2005. The full version of this document, which offers additional advice on creating a document assembly project, is available at www.capstonepractice.com/s/keys.pdf.

No two document assembly projects are the same, even within the same organization. Here are some of the ways projects differ. Where does yours fit?

USERS

Who are the intended users of the application? Lawyers, paralegals, secretaries, students, clients? Are they experts in the area in question, or novices? Are they a few or many? Do they work in proximity, or are they spread among floors, offices, or cities?

DOCUMENTS

What documents is the system designed to produce? Short and simple, long and complex, or somewhere in between? Are they typically first draft-final, or do they require lots of post-assembly editing? Are official, graphical forms involved? Are the documents typically produced individually, or in related sets? Can they be neatly handled with fill-in-the-blanks variables and alternative/additional passages, or do they involve lots of material that doesn't lend itself to straight-forward rules?

SCOPE

What range of transactions is the system intended to support? How deep do you intend to go in modeling the variations from transaction to transaction? Is the system designed only to produce first drafts, or guide users through several stages of revision and negotiation? Should it offer project management and decision support features?

PURPOSES

What are the driving goals of the application? To speed up processing? Improve quality or consistency? Achieve greater capacity? Allow work to be delegated to more efficient staffing levels? Assist in training?

NOVELTY

Is this the organization's first effort of this kind, or one among several? Are the team members experienced in this kind of thing? There are vast differences between doing a first project of this kind and later ones. They involve different states of organizational and personal readiness.

STAFFING

Is the project being done entirely with in-house personnel, by an outside consultant, or some blend? Is it conceived as a project by lawyers in a practice group, aided by others, or as an initiative of the IT department, aided by lawyers?

* * *

Marc Lauritsen is the founder and president of Capstone Practice Systems. He practiced law and supervised in legal

*services programs and then served as an instructor, direc-
tor of clinical programs, and a senior research associate
at Harvard Law School. He currently serves as an adjunct
professor at Suffolk University Law School. Marc is one
of the godfathers of the legal tech movement, as well as a
world-renowned expert on document assembly systems. He
can be reached by email at marc@capstonepractice.com.*

* * *

EMERGING TRENDS IN LEGAL KNOWLEDGE DELIVERY MODELS

When my team and I founded Afterpattern (then known as Community.lawyer) in 2016, our vision was to build a platform that made it easy for legal professionals to transform their expertise into products. Today we're seeing exactly what we had hoped—thousands of law firms scaling their expertise to new heights with software—but also something we never anticipated: the emergence of unexpected and entirely new categories of legal products. Let me highlight some examples to explain—starting with the kind of product we *did* expect.

CLIENT PRODUCTS

When Afterpattern first launched our App Builder platform, the core use case we envisioned was law firms using the web apps they built to serve more clients more affordably—primarily, by creating automations for intake and document drafting.

For example, Siskind Susser PC—one of the largest immigration law firms in North America—has used Afterpattern to create an online toolkit to help hospitals navigate the complex regulations that govern the hiring of medical doctors from abroad. For every potential hire by a hospital, the law firm used to have to sit down with the hospital's HR team, ask pages of questions, and then use that information to manually draft a report analyzing whether the hire was permissible and, if not, the remedial steps the hospital needed to take.

Today, the firm's clients can simply go to an online portal, answer a branching-logic questionnaire, and automatically generate the report. The beauty of the automation is that not only does it eliminate manual processes that used to take hours and hours of firm labor—but productizing this expertise has allowed Siskind Susser to dramatically expand their addressable market from the dozens of hospitals they had the staffing for to now *any hospital in the country.*

PUBLIC PRODUCTS

Is it really possible for a law firm to outcompete LegalZoom by, for example, building a tool to incorporate a business? The answer is probably "no." LegalZoom and companies like it are frighteningly good at creating and, crucially, *marketing* DIY legal products that service large, often national markets. But the answer to the question above is beside the point. LegalZoom may have the market for generic/federal DIY legal products cornered—but legal experts have advantages that let them build DIY products LegalZoom can't or won't. These fall into two buckets in our experience: quick response apps and local apps.

Quick response apps are ones that are released days or even hours after a change in the law—a kind of nimbleness that behemoths like LegalZoom often aren't equipped for. For example, at the beginning of the Covid-19 pandemic and a few short days after California announced a moratorium on evictions, a scrappy team of nonprofits used Afterpattern to launch www.norent.org, a tool that enables tenants in Los Angeles to provide their landlord with the written notification required to avail themselves of this new protection. The app saw hundreds of uses within the first 48 hours.

Another type of DIY product that legal experts are well-positioned to create are those that leverage the expert's understanding of local areas of law. For a company the size of LegalZoom to invest in launching a new product—e.g., to identify a legal need, hire an expert to design a solution, and build out a custom web application to implement that solution—the financial return has to be on the order of seven figures at a minimum. But for a law firm that already understands the solution to a legal need in their community based on knowledge they already cultivate for their own practice, the cost of launching this product is much lower—especially when deployed using affordable, no-code platforms like Afterpattern. And unlike LegalZoom, many law firms wouldn't sniff at a new six-figure revenue stream.

LAWYER-TO-LAWYER PRODUCTS

The most novel type of legal product we've seen emerge on our platform is what we call "lawyer-to-lawyer" apps: ones that legal experts make available directly to other lawyers to leverage in their own practices. What's interesting about this category of product is it's actually a meta-category: Once a legal expert builds something for their own firm, that expert can easily turn around and market that same product to other lawyers, too.

Remember Siskind Susser, the immigration firm that built an online toolkit to help hospitals hire foreign doctors? Later this year, they plan to make that product and a suite of others available for any immigration law firm to use in their own practice with their own clients. That means a solo immigration attorney anywhere in America will be able to power their practice using a workflow built and maintained by top immigration experts. We've seen this same pattern play out repeatedly on our platform. A legal aid organization builds a triage tool that other legal aid providers can now duplicate and customize for their own use. A small law firm in Missouri creates a client intake for their estates practice and offers it on a subscription basis to other firms.

At Afterpattern, we've realized the enormous potential of this emerging expertise delivery model and have engineered our platform to make "lawyer-to-lawyer" subscription products as easy as possible to launch. In just a few clicks, legal experts can now take the product they built to solve their own service delivery bottleneck and offer it on a subscription basis to literally any legal professional in the world. In this way, we're seeing the expertise bottleneck gradually disappear, app by app.

* * *

Scott Kelly is the president of Afterpattern, a platform that law firms use to turn their expertise into software products. Selected as one of Clio's top integrations, Afterpattern is used by thousands of legal professionals across the world. Scott can be reached at scott@afterpattern.com.

Triage and Referral

Triage and referral help legal professionals better handle the administrative work of running a legal organization. These tools can be productized as back-end tools. For example, imagine an administrator at a major university's campus legal services office. The administrator spends a large portion of the day taking phone calls from the public, writing down their issue, entering their information into an Excel spreadsheet, deciding which lawyer should receive the referral (based on issue, geographic region, and who is owed a referral next), then coordinating an introduction between the lawyer and client. By transforming this service into a product, the admin can focus their time on things like marketing their service, recruiting new attorneys, etc.

Another way to use a triage and referral system is to handle client intakes. Consider a personal injury firm that spends a great deal of time screening calls from potential clients, many of which are not colorable claims because the statute of limitations has passed or it is clear there is no liability for the incident that could be alleged against anyone else. A firm with an intake tool that could qualify claims by confirming they occurred within the limitations period and within the jurisdiction would help cut down on time a human paralegal might spend on the phone with the same people. If the claim appeared to be colorable, the tool could then ask for basic information to contact the client and seek permission to have an attorney call them. A slightly more sophisticated version of this tool could triage claims between levels of promise they offer, then have partners call on the cases with the biggest potential, senior associates on medium potential, and rookie attorneys on cases that seem marginal. As an added bonus, these triage and referral tools can help gather data so that, over time, their efficiency can be maximized by identifying trends from the matters that come in through them.

Conceptually, this sort of tool will most commonly take the form of a guided interview that gathers the information users put in, then either gathers the information organizers put in for a human to more easily deal with or uses expert system "rules" to do so automatically (e.g., it could send all matters the user indicated involve a contract to Attorney A, and all matters that involve a tort claim to Attorney B. It could copy the general counsel on all referrals so that she can oversee her team and keep a summary of information in a spreadsheet so the team can gather data and spot trends).

CALCULATORS

Some calculations are challenging for anyone but experienced professionals to make. Internally, it's niche knowledge for professionals to create formulas to help them do their work more efficiently. These can be formulas to help with investment planning, tools that help best structure annuities to avoid undue taxes, or tools that calculate the amount due to various parties for a medical lien.

The value of these tools is that they make (presumably complex) calculations simple, often using a proprietary formula to help guide decision-making. To develop one requires its creator to understand a complex formula that would be valuable to end users if packaged into a simple tool that allowed the user to plug information when cued to do so. Turning a calculator into a product requires very little tech skill because basic calculators can be created using simple spreadsheet software. Versions beyond the working prototype may require front-end development skill so they have an attractive appearance. There aren't many channels for selling calculators, but one can link to them from a personal website and either sell access there or use it to drive traffic to the site.

DATA

Products fueled by data and machine learning can provide powerful ways to meet users' needs. From tools that use data to make medical predictions to tools that use data to predict how a judge will behave in a given situation, such tools nowadays often use machine learning to develop predictive models.

In some ways, data products are not stand-alone tools, but instead add value to other tools. For example, it is efficient to use document assembly to automate often-repeated contracts, but far more attractive to make a document assembly system that then is capable of reporting which clauses are most likely to lead to litigation when the system is used at scale. For this reason, creating a productized service that relies on data will typically be a heavier lift than other forms or productization, because it necessarily requires a combination of tech-savviness and the ability to apply mathematical methods to make something of the information fueling the product. While the barrier to entry to making data products is dropping, this chiefly remains the domain of data scientists with coding expertise.

In some instances, companies and firms have had data scientists on staff for other purposes and then used them as in-house consultants to help build out their product. For example, Littler Mendelsohn hired a national director of data analytics to help clients develop and implement legally compliant data analytic approaches to analyzing case-filings.[7] Littler also began to analyze its own data and statistical issues that arose from representing clients. It has subsequently spun this knowledge into a product, Littler CaseSmart, that provides data tracking and reporting as well as benchmarking. These resources

---

7. https://www.littler.com/publication-press/press/littler-hires-its-first-national-director-data-analytics-and-launches-data.

offer insights that would never be available without a data product built to identify them:

> We track hundreds of data points related to every matter and serve them up to you via a secure, web-based dashboard. What is the average lifecycle of your matters from open to close? In which jurisdictions do you experience more litigation? What are your average fees per case? What is your average settlement of a charge, and how does that compare to other organizations? With 24-7 access to these key performance indicators (KPIs) and so much more, you will have a clear picture of the trends taking place within your organization, allowing your team to make more informed business decisions.[8]

Littler's development of an internal data shop and data product required a major institutional investment. While creating a data product may be the realm of big shops with big budgets, that needn't be the only case. For example, imagine a personal injury attorney who gathers data on the discounts that she is able to negotiate with lienholders in cases: Insurer A will always agree to between a 20 and 40 percent lien reduction based on 100 negotiations, whereas Insurer B will only agree to a 10 percent reduction unless the value of the lien exceeds the value of the settlement, in which case they will reduce it by 50 percent. This sort of product could be created and updated with little more than a spreadsheet and a willingness to provide others with regular updates.

*   *   *

With those categories as a starting point, your mind may be starting to whir with ideas for products will be the best fit for you to build. To focus your approach, chapter 4 will guide you through creating a hypothesis around the people you want to help and the problem you want to solve.

---

8. https://www.littler.com/service-solutions/littler-casesmart.

Exercise: Survey the Field

The best way to get a sense for the types of productized services is to experience them first-hand.

Get on the web and identify at least one example in each category. Even for those behind a paywall, in almost all instances you should be able to get a sneak peak of what the authors created and how it works (if you don't have direct access to the tool, try searching YouTube to see if there are online demos of it).

Reflection Questions

What qualities or attributes are common among different types of productized services? What other types of products not mentioned in this chapter share those same attributes?

Part II

A Process for Productizing Legal Work

Now that you have a basic understanding of the role and dynamics of productizing legal services, you are ready to learn about the process of productizing a service. Each chapter in Part II describes a stage in that process. Using introductory text, examples, anecdotes from experts in the field, and hands-on exercises for developing skills and deepening understanding, readers will better understand how one can create productized legal services and can learn an approach for doing so on their own.

Chapter 4

Begin by Assessing Your Resources and Goals

L et's take a step back from chapter 3's view of productized services as bits and bytes, automation, or AI, and look at the ways a productized service is a *business*, or at least a new branch of an existing business.

Consider the accountant who begins selling an amortization calculator, or the financial advisor who creates a newsletter on some market niche. Both are doing something quite different from most of their workaday counterparts. They are both creating new streams of revenue that will require them to adapt their skills and expand their knowledge to branch out into new areas of business (in this case, sales and publishing). The accountant may need to assemble a sales force to promote the amortization calculator. The financial advisor may need to create listservs and use social media to expand the reach of the newsletter. Ideally, they both have anticipated these factors as integral to their productization process.

Likewise, before you productize a service—create a new business—you should consider what you will need to know or do to support the success of that product. Will you have adequate resources at your disposal? Without the expertise, skills, and resources you'll need, your project may never get off the ground (or if it does, you may not be able to keep it going for very long). The first part of this chapter addresses these questions as a preliminary step in the process of productizing.

Moreover, whether you *can* do something is different from whether you *should* do something. As a prerequisite to productizing a service, you ought to consider what function productizing this service plays in your own plans. Are you motivated by challenge and personal growth? Are you motivated by money? The public interest . . . ? Ultimately, only you know the answers, but reflecting on these questions is an important step before conceptualizing, testing, and building a tangible thing. It is important to honestly assess what you hope to get out of a project before investing a great deal of time, energy, and resources in it.

DETERMINING YOUR CAPABILITIES

One of the best ways to tell whether an entrepreneurial venture is bound for success is the self-efficacy of its creator.[1] In other words, *does the person at the helm have confidence that they can be successful in their work?* Researchers at Northwestern University's Kellogg School of Management have used several thousand survey responses to arrive at three core questions that correspond to three specific areas of focus that someone making a productized service should consider.

1. Overall, Will My Skills and Abilities Help Me on This Project?

This question maps onto the question of what technology will go into building the productized service. As the next section will detail, productizing runs the gamut: from a nearly no-tech, fully paper-based resource (like a newsletter) to a full-blown app requiring full-stack development skills. While selecting a project, it makes sense to ask whether you have the skills required to build it.

WHAT IF I DON'T HAVE STRONG TECH SKILLS?

You don't need strong tech skills to create a *minimum viable product* (MVP). An MVP is an early prototype or

---

1. https://qz.com/work/1332019/3-questions-all-inspiring-entrepreneurs-should -ask-themselves/.

test version of a product, with just enough features to give end users a taste for the finished product that you aspire to build once you have gathered enough investors and resources to pull it off. Many tools are available that enable laypeople (who don't have mad tech skills) to create MVPs to test out their ideas. So, before dismissing an ambitious idea as too high-tech for you, consider building an MVP to test the waters. It could motivate you to acquire more tech skills, or to hire others to transform your MVP into a professional-grade product.

Second, for some people, in some organizations, tech resources exist that would allow for a more significant investment of resources at the bat, even if the person at the helm of the project has no skills whatsoever. If a colleague codes, or there is an internal fund available to hire coders, it may be that professionals can be involved with the process from the outset.

2. Will My Past Experiences Be Valuable in Helping Me Execute This Project?

This issue maps to the question of *expertise*. Put differently: Are you a wizard at the thing you want to productize?

No one will want to watch a 20-hour online course on how to manage a trusts-and-estates practice from someone with no experience succeeding in such a role. So unless you *are* a person with vast expertise across a given area, it makes more sense to develop a productized service that directly relates to your expertise and your strengths. In recent years, researchers have posited the "long tail theory"[2] of the Internet, which suggests that deep knowledge of a specific, obscure area is what is most valuable as a product. Even

---

2. For the definitive take on the long tail phenomenon, check out Chris Anderson's *The Long Tail: Why the Future of Business is Selling Less of More* (Boston: Hachette Book Group, 2008).

if you are the recognized expert in a space, it might make sense to focus more narrowly.

From my own experience practicing law, I can attest to this: I worked in a litigation law firm, where part of the challenge of closing any case was determining which liens asserted against the value of our case had to be resolved for full price, which could be negotiated, and which did not require attention at all. It was a total mess. It brought no value to the case, either. (It was the client's money we had to distribute—a necessary service, but not one that brought us more payment for doing it correctly.) I became an expert in this arcane, complex field. Before long, I was training others, partners with decades of experience were coming to me with questions, and I was answering questions on listservs and building a personal brand. This was an important lesson: It's hard to be good at the big thing in a given industry (being the lead trial lawyer, making the cuts in a surgery, developing the custom investment plan), but it's relatively easy to become a trusted resource on a narrow subskill of "the big thing."

3. Am I Confident I Can Put in the Time and Effort Necessary to Succeed on This Project?

This query largely speaks for itself, but that doesn't mean it's not worthy of real consideration. Before embarking on a project, spend some time thinking about your time and energy and your ability to combine a new project with other important priorities (whether professional or personal). How much time can you invest in creating it? And just as importantly, how much time can you spend on maintaining or updating it?

Some things are inherently quick hitters and can be accomplished in very few steps. For example, summarizing your expertise on a specific topic and posting it online for a webinar is a pretty simple process. Getting other projects off the ground, however, can become a full-time job. And some projects, like a newsletter, are not that hard to get started but will continue to require regular maintenance. (No one subscribes to a newsletter that's published at random intervals.) So, before creating your product, honestly assess whether you have the time required to get it started and whether you'll continue to have time (or access to human resources) to keep your product going, growing, timely, and competitive into the foreseeable future.

So how much time and energy should you plan on investing in productizing? Generally speaking, the simplest answer for larger scale projects is *a lot*. There's a reason that Silicon Valley CEOs tell stories about sleeping under their desks and ordering takeout for every meal in the early years in the life of a start-up.

Big projects take not just a lot of time, they take a lot *more* time than what you're likely imagining. Some of that time will be spent doing busy work, like connecting with people on LinkedIn to ask them to chat about your project or creating mailing lists so you can send out one-pagers (a one-page pitch or overview of your product). But the lion's share will be spent coding and debugging, or drafting and revising, or testing and retesting, as you grind through the process of developing your ideas into a product, a business plan, and a marketing strategy. You'll need to invest lots of time on all the many different aspects of productizing.

To work effectively, you'll have to invest your prime time—those hours of the day when you are sharp and focused. This use of your time may have implications for other aspects of your life. For example, if your project takes time away from billable hours at your firm, who is going to make them up?

Beyond work obligations, you should also consider the impact of a prospective project on your home life. Discuss your proposed plans with the people who will be affected most directly. Be candid about the fact that your project will mean spending less time with the kids, or less time with your partner, or less time contributing to housekeeping and home repairs, or all of the above. In the short term, maybe you will make less money. Perhaps the long-term benefits could justify some short-term sacrifices, but is your risk tolerance the same as your partner's? In the interest of garnering support and preserving the peace, these are all matters that should be discussed early and honestly before you embark on any big project.

* * *

The idea is that you should not select a project unless you can answer "yes" to all three of the above questions. This applies to your first project, and every project thereafter: *Whenever* considering a new project, you can map it back to these three questions: Do I have the subject matter expertise (and gravitas) to pull this project off? *Do I have access to the tech knowledge to make it work? Do I have the time and capacity to launch this and keep it afloat?* If the answer is yes to all three, there's a potential match, and it's time to take the next step.

ASSESSING YOUR RISK TOLERANCE

Once you have a sense of what you *can* build, it makes sense to analyze whether you *should* build it. Specifically, you should consider what goals you are trying to achieve and how much risk you can assume to achieve them.

What Are Your Goals and Aspirations?

The answer to the question *"What should I productize?"* depends, in part, on your personal and professional goals as the creator. If you aspire to turn your project into a full-time job, such as building a data-harvesting app, you will probably need to suspend your current professional path and dive into your project full-time, with both feet.

On the other hand, if you want to take on work as an added revenue stream, a side hustle, or to make your industry or community a better place, then you want to consider projects that are relatively light touch, like a webinar, simple calculator, or newsletter. For these types of projects, you can take an easier approach to answering the big questions about your goals and aspirations, because they generally involve less time and lower risk.

If you're close to the brass ring of achieving partner at your law firm, you might want to reconsider the wisdom of working up a business plan that includes a request to devote one-third of your billable hours to a new venture.

If you are unwilling to leave your current job to run a new app that you've created (an app that may require you to work 80 hours per week), you may need to consider abandoning the app in favor of a less time-consuming project or explore alternative ways to make your new app work (for example, by partnering with others who could share the work of developing it).

The flip side of thinking about what you *want* to happen on a given project is considering how prepared you are to deal with the consequences if it goes wrong. In the next section, we'll see how the success or failure of a product does not have to determine whether its creator emerges as a winner or loser.

MacGuffins Have Value, Too

If you're a movie buff, you'll recall that in *Pulp Fiction* the characters Jules and Vincent spend their time pursuing a mysterious, glowing briefcase—contents unknown. If you're more into classics, you might remember that in the *Maltese Falcon*, starring the iconic private investigator played by Humphrey Bogart, the film's characters are chasing after a golden bird statue. Here's the kicker about the briefcase in *Pulp Fiction* and the bird statue in *The Maltese Falcon*: They don't really matter. Yes, they propel the films' action, but not because of what the suitcase contains or the value of the bird. If Jules and Vincent had been holding a golden bird, and Bogey had been pursuing a glowing suitcase, it would not alter any of the important features of those classics. The suitcase and Maltese falcon are what film school types call *MacGuffins*. A MacGuffin is an object, idea, person, or goal that the characters are motivated by. What the MacGuffin *is* is not important except as a device to give action and reveal something about the character.

In a perfect world, building a new tool or product would make a direct and positive impact. But what if it doesn't? Is it necessarily a failure?

In short, no. The thing that you build can be a MacGuffin: Every aspect of building it can promote your professional growth and increase your self-awareness. Maybe, like the Maltese falcon, it doesn't turn out to be solid gold, but the process of productizing it may enrich you nonetheless.

By completing the productizing process (even one that doesn't find a market), you will learn more about:

- The legal industry
- How to identify problems and use modern tools to solve try to solve them
- The efforts that others have previously made to solve the problems you've identified

- How to connect with peers, mentors, and clients to talk about their problems and how to solve them
- How to prototype a solution, test it, and improve it
- How to think about what it means to bring new revenue streams or opportunities to your existing organization and what impact that can have
- A framework for creatively solving business challenges in the future

If you are offered the opportunity to do any of the above, choosing to participate will likely be a wise investment of your time and energy. By going through the productization process, or just thinking about it while reading this book, you can learn a great deal regardless of whether the product succeeds or fails on its merits. From learning about the productizing process, you see that there is always the potential to create something that could help many people and maybe even boost your own future prospects as well.

Making Things Can Lead to Other, Sometimes Unexpected, Good Things

Building a product can also lead to all sorts of unexpected positives that grow in unpredictable ways from the project itself.

Have you heard about Slack? It's a communication tool that combines the best of text messages and email. Like most people in my circle, I use Slack daily to stay in contact with colleagues, students, and collaborators with whom I work on various projects. I even have a Slack channel with my college roommates, where we chat about work and life and share pictures of our kids doing silly things.

Here's the surprising thing about Slack: It wasn't intended to be a billion-dollar, stand-alone company called Slack.[3] The team that built Slack set out to build a video game called *Glitch*. (Have you ever heard of a video game called *Glitch*? Nor had I. *Glitch* was a modestly successful online game that lots of people could play simultaneously.)

---

3. https://www.theguardian.com/small-business-network/2016/jul/18/slack-co-founder-happy-accident-1bn-startup.

The builders of *Glitch* set out to create a tool that would allow their entire team, which was spread out in offices from San Francisco to Vancouver, to communicate with each other as a group easily and in real time. Along with programmers, they wanted their artists, animators, and sound designers to be involved in the development process. The idea was for everyone to collaborate, swap assets, and be notified as things progressed. In essence, the *tool* they created for the purpose of building a game, *Glitch*, became the product and the name of a very successful company, Slack.

And the game they intended to create? *Glitch*? It died quietly about a year after it was launched.

HOW JULIE SAVARINO PRODUCTIZES HER WORK

I was raised by entrepreneurs, so thinking about ways to monetize my work and scale my business by turning services into products was ingrained in me in childhood.

When it comes to developing my next product, one technique I've found helpful is to formally schedule a time twice a year to take a step back and reflect upon what I've worked on lately or during the preceding year. While I do this, I am asking myself the question "What can I re-sell next year that I did this year (or recently)?" This helps me both reflect on the things I've accomplished and proactively think about how I can leverage the hard work I've already done to add value to my client and their firms and to help more lawyers and professionals in the future.

This sort of thinking helped me create the "Marketing Partner Forum" in 1992. When I came up with the idea, I'd been consulting with law firms all over the world, helping them devise and implement strategies and tactics to generate new business. It struck me that if I could gather these clients together in one room, it would not only make a better learning opportunity for them but would allow them to learn from one another and create a valuable network for them. Plus, it was more efficient for me to invite them all to one location at the same time instead of me visiting each of them individually. So the Marketing Partner Forum was a win-win-win for my clients, for me, and for my business. It became an annual event, resulting in a successful acquisition eight years after I started it. It's still going strong now, several decades later.

I continue to regularly look for ways to add value to, reuse, leverage, monetize, and productize my work. For example, for years I accumulated vast amounts of how-to info on effectively selling legal and professional services. About 20 years ago, I compiled it all into a series of sales support checklists to help lawyers prepare when they are seeking or pitching new business. My clients really liked these checklists because they helped save time, improved results, and provided valuable sales training and coaching content.

So I thought to myself: How else could this content be delivered in a way that will be useful for my clients? I converted them into an app, called the Rainmaker Coach App on iTunes. The app gives users immediate access to information and tools that help make the most of time spent trying to develop new business.

Then, a few years later, I re-converted the checklist and app information into another product: a book on Amazon. It's called *Master-Level Business & Client Development Activity Checklists*. The reality was, once I'd created the checklists and app products, creating another product out of the content in the form of a book was relatively simple. These products allowed me to help more lawyers and other professionals and have also led to new referrals and other new business because more lawyers, law firm marketers, and other professionals became aware of me, my services, expertise, and the results I help generate.

* * *

Julie Savarino is a leading, award-winning business/client development, client service, value and experience strategist, and coach for lawyers, law firms, and legal departments.

She holds an MBA and a JD, is a licensed attorney, and has successfully served in-house in client and business development positions for the law firms of Dickinson Wright and Butzel Long and for the accounting firm Grant Thornton. Julie can be reached at julie@busdevinc.com.

Like All Good Things in Life, It's Subject to Change

New information and life changes can necessitate a revised analysis of your resources, your risk tolerance, and even your goals and aspirations.

If the pilot of your new productized service exceeds your expectations, perhaps it's time to consider taking a chance, and either quitting your job or asking for time off from work to take your project over the finish line.

On the other hand, if you have a new baby on the way, or a new mortgage, or your spouse just lost their job, maybe you don't want to put your current employment at risk. Maybe you would even consider scaling back the time you have been putting into your project and refocus your ambitions toward a possible promotion.

The important thing to realize is that you can and will return to these questions over and over again in the course of your life. You will make decisions based on the dynamic conditions of living, your personal and professional goals, and the potential opportunities presented by your product. There is no single right answer to any of these questions, nor any perfect way to predict outcomes. But it is a valuable exercise and an important preliminary step to consider all of these issues before getting in too deep.

Exercise: Brief Bio

Who *are* you? What are you interested in and what problems in the world would you like to solve? A generation of MBA students and future executives have taken the Meyers-Briggs test and completed other self-assessment tools to think about how they think about the world. Here, we want to do something slightly different, though in the same spirit.

Part 1

In one paragraph each, answer the following questions:

1. What is something in your professional life that you have deep knowledge in, such that others would rely on you for advice on it?
2. How capable are you of building something that requires technology, either personally or based on access to others who would assist?
3. What capacity do you have to build and maintain a new project?
4. What is personal success to you?
5. What is personal failure to you?

Part 2

Now, after you have written responses to those questions, convert that self-assessment into the opening page of a portfolio to serve as your mission statement. Later on, you'll use this bio to help you establish credibility with investors or others who have the capacity to greenlight your project.

In two or three sentences, tell your audience (a) an area you have deep knowledge in, (b) the background or experience that would give others a basis for using the productized service you've created, and (c), as appropriate, information about your tech chops that suggest your ability to lead a productization project.

Example: Imagine that Jayne Jones is a lawyer seeking funding from her firm's development committee to turn her expertise in working up dental malpractice cases into a webinar series. She believes that this will both help to train newer attorneys and serve as a way to establish herself as her community's top resource for referring this type of cases. Her bio might read:

Jayne Jones has 25 years of experience as an attorney focused in the area of dental malpractice. She has served as lead counsel in 40 jury trials and has served as past chair of the state bar's malpractice section. In the past, she has created successful continuing legal education chapters to share this expertise that have been read by over 5,000 local attorneys.

Chapter 5

Identify Problems, Then Work Backward

WHAT'S THE PURPOSE OF A MILKSHAKE?

The answer to this question can be surprisingly nuanced and relevant to the work of product development.[1]

> Among the best anecdotes of the late, great Harvard business professor, Clayton Christensen, is his story of a fast-food restaurant chain that wanted to improve its milkshake sales. The company tried to accomplish this with a survey that asked milkshake drinkers to describe their perfect milkshake. Responding to their customers' feedback, the company tried to create the perfect milkshake. But still their sales did not improve. The company then enlisted the help of one of Christensen's colleagues.
>
> Christensen's colleague approached the situation by trying to deduce the "job" that customers were "hiring" a milkshake to do. The researcher spent a day in one of the restaurants, documenting who was buying milkshakes, when they bought them, and whether or not they drank their milkshake on the premises. The researcher discovered that of the milkshakes purchased first thing in the morning, 40 percent of customers (who were commuters) had ordered them to go.

---

1. https://hbswk.hbs.edu/item/clay-christensens-milkshake-marketing.

The following day, he returned in the morning to inter-view the customers who were buying their milkshakes to go. Most of them told him they faced a long, boring drive to work. They needed something to keep their hands busy to make the commute more interesting. They said they weren't hungry at the time they purchased the milkshake, but they knew they would be later, so they wanted something to stave off their hunger until lunch. Moreover, they were in a hurry, they were in work clothes, and they needed at least one hand free for the steering wheel. The milkshake was self-contained and tidy. It satisfied their appetites and drinking it through the straw gave the customers something to do while they drove.

The reasons why customers on their way to work in the morning "hire" the milkshake instead of a bagel or a donut become obvious when viewed in this light: What is the job that the milkshake is being hired to do?

Once the company understood the job (or purpose) of the milkshake, it could respond more by creating a *morning milkshake* that was even thicker (to last through a long commute) and more interesting (with chunks of fruit) than its predecessor. Furthermore, the company made similar adjustments to other milkshakes being routinely purchased by customers at other times (afternoon, evening) and for other jobs. A parent bringing a child to get a milkshake directly after school to celebrate a good report card is "hir-ing" that milkshake to do a very different "job" than that of the commuting worker's milkshake. At 3:30 in the afternoon, a thinner milkshake would make sense, so as not to spoil everyone's appetite for supper in two or three hours.

* * *

In chapter 4, we discussed the need to develop a clear sense of what your goals are before embarking on a big project. In chapter 3, we surveyed different types and forms of productized services and work. We've looked at a number of examples that have already been devel-oped. The next step in productizing is to figure out whether your customers ultimately will buy a milkshake, and to do so, you must have an understanding of what void it will fill in their lives.

Building a Better "Milkshake" in the Legal Profession

There's a bit of good news here for those who already have experience in the legal profession. With typical startups, founders are building something from scratch to serve a need they perceive in the world. Those who work in law offices already have a grasp of the many jobs that are ongoing in that environment. This gives you, a person who is developing a productized service for the legal profession, a couple of big advantages over, say, someone else who is looking to invent something that never existed before in an industry they've only examined from the outside.

The Advantages of Working from Within

First, productized services created by insiders to an industry are already partially validated, in a sense, when they are typically already offered as old-fashioned services. Put differently, people who offer a service in the traditional one-to-one fashion know whether there is a market of people who would use that service. Contrast this with the situation where a person creates an altogether new tool, website, or business with the hope that it will create a new market. This requires a lot of research, and some faith too, that their research and hunches are correct. In contrast, with productized services, we know the need exists, because people are already paying a lot of money to fulfill it in its traditional "service" form.

When productizing for an *existing* service, the focus is on whether target users would be willing to *substitute* that service for your productized version. Sometimes, switching to the productized service is a no brainer for your target user. For example, the choice between paying an estate attorney to handle a will or using an online form to create a legal will at a fraction of the cost is a clear one. But sometimes, the decision to switch to the productized service won't be so cut-and-dried. Consider the choice between a software system created by expert psychotherapists in which the target user answers questions about their feelings online and traditional in-person talk therapy.

When you know that your target user needs the service and is willing to pay for it, your goal in productizing the existing service is to adapt it to achieve greater efficiency compared to the traditional form, and then to use that efficiency advantage to offer more value to the end user than the traditional service can provide.

To return to the milkshake example, this is the work of taking an already popular product and thinking about how best to package it to do the job that the customer needs done and then doing that job with greater efficiency. In subsequent chapters, you'll learn about a method for testing your hypotheses to confirm that they are in line with your target user's needs and desires.

Second, if you're already working in the legal field or have access to collaborators who are, it's likely that you will have a leg up because you come to productization with an understanding of the content that has already been created for internal use in the legal environment and that has the potential to be productized. For example, if a paralegal has already written a set of instructions intended to train peers in the use of automation tools, it makes sense to consider using that information as the starting point for a product dealing with the same core of information. For those working within a firm or professional organization, it also makes sense to poll colleagues to see what information they have collected or created that could be repurposed. For example, a paper intake form could be automated and posted on a website; instructions for a complex calculation used to settle cases could be built into a simple app; or a collection of contract clauses could be made searchable and shareable more efficiently.

But having access to content and information is not, on its own, all that you'll need to start creating a productized service. One must start at the *end* by asking "For whom will this tool be made, and what *job* do they need this tool to do (more efficiently)?"

START AT THE END: TARGET A USER WITH A SPECIFIC PROBLEM

Many bad products would never have been made had their creators kept better focus on their intended end user. Put differently, making the world's best app or online course is only meaningful if there are end users for whom it solves a problem. With productized services, the question is whether the solution you're providing will deliver the same value (or close to it) to the end user but with some added benefit that would dissuade them from just going to a brick-and-mortar provider to resolve their issue. That added benefit can be reduced cost, increased efficiency, more privacy, or more convenient access (like a website or calculator that works 24 hours a day, not just during business hours).

While solving a specific problem for the target user can help the target user, however, it can create problems for collateral others who should be considered as well. For example, who hasn't dialed a toll-free number to get help with a confusing bill or broken cable TV, only to be forced to answer a number of questions generated by a robotic voice? And beyond that, who hasn't thought to themselves, "If only this company had a human operator pick up on the first ring, I'd be a happier customer, and my problem would get solved a lot sooner!" It's a tradeoff. Taking the company's perspective, the automated-voice answering service likely saves the company money. The company has also probably calculated that the number of frustrated callers they will lose as customers will be offset by the money the company saves on human resources. But clearly, the customer's expectation of excellent customer service isn't met when a company focuses entirely on improving its bottom line. We can reduce the negatives in this tradeoff by following a good process, but we should never lose sight of the fact that by productizing certain things, we may be creating other challenges. On balance, it may be that the value of solving the original problem is sufficient to outweigh the detriment of any new problems created, but that shouldn't be taken for granted as true in every case.

Later on, we'll test out whether our idea matches with an actual need. Here, we will begin to create a hypothesis that will be built on in subsequent chapters. When considering a new project, start by creating a target user. Ask yourself the questions explored in the following sections.

For What Specific Group of People Do You Envision Building?

Who is most likely to make use of the productized service? Get granular here. Just listing "other lawyers," "clients," or "judges" is too broad. Think about their common characteristics, including demographics and behavior. Instead of "lawyers," try "residential real estate attorneys who do closings in Massachusetts." Start by envisioning solutions for a narrow group, and over time, a successful product may have enough features to add value that may have enough features to expand its reach. Best to begin with a more laser-like focus, though.

What Problem Do You Believe This Target User Has That Needs a Solution?

If the target users do not have a problem in need of solving, there is no need to build something new to solve it. Get specific here, too, in terms of the challenge you envision the target users face. In the previous section, we envisioned Massachusetts residential real estate attorneys who do closings. Perhaps a serious problem among this community is the time wasted standing in long lines at the registry of deeds to file papers. Again, we want to be granular here: Saying "wasted time" is too broad. We want to build a specific solution, for a specific class of end users, so defining their problem narrowly is just as important as defining them narrowly.

Why Is Your Solution So Much Better Than the Traditional "Service" Offering That People Will Switch to Your Product?

Since productized services come in so many flavors, this question will have many possible answers. If you're offering a truly new product—a calculator that doesn't already exist but that can make a lawyer's life easier, or a webinar to train in-house counsel on analyzing proposals from law firms—you're breaking new ground and there's unlikely to be a competitor from whom you're drawing business.

Much of the process this book teaches is derived from the discipline of "design thinking." Those wishing to take a deeper dive should look into the work of the Stanford Legal Design Lab, as well as IDEO.org. Design thinking wonks might think of this as "out of order." Typically, the design thinking process first asks adherents to "empathize," i.e., do a whole bunch of user interviews, before attempting

If your product, by contrast, fits into a category with existing tools (and you just have a strategy to do it *better*), the analysis will be different. That is the subject of the next chapter.

to define a problem. However, the design thinking process is made to be nonlinear, and given legal professionals' close contact with their clients and peers, it makes more sense in this case to hypothesize a solution before getting too deeply involved in time-consuming interviews.

INSIGHTS ON UNDERSTANDING CLIENT PROBLEMS FROM MIKE CAPPUCCI, PARTNER AT FOUNDATIONLAB

Truly understand client problems before pursuing solutions. This cannot be overstated. Consumers are not actively searching for your product. They are seeking better outcomes in one or more aspects of their human experience. Those desired outcomes exist with or without your product. Identify moments of friction or the obstacles preventing your clients from reaching their desired outcomes. That's where real product opportunities lay.

You believe you have, based on your experience working with your clients, a strong understanding of their desired outcomes. You may be right. But it's also possible you're only seeing a piece of the puzzle. Clients are complicated. And they often accept minimally satisfactory outcomes from professionals they trust.

"People don't want to buy a quarter-inch drill. They want a quarter-inch hole!"[2] An immigration lawyer who helps clients fill out necessary forms to file for citizenship could rationalize the completion of the form as the desired outcome for their client. But is that really the reason why they engaged the lawyer? No—they want citizenship. Or better yet, ask: Why do they want citizenship in the first place?

---

2. https://hbswk.hbs.edu/item/what-customers-want-from-your-products.

An actionable step to do this is to ask your clients to **SHOW** you their problems, not tell you about them. You can do this by gathering anecdotal evidence: "Tell me a story about the last time you tried to accomplish X." Better still, ask to see emails, texts with friends, notes they've written that really capture the moments of friction. From there, you can infer their true desired outcomes and the obstacles they face. If nothing else, the above tactics will put the client in the right headspace to discuss their challenges more openly and accurately.

Before turning your focus to product and choosing which features to prioritize, make sure you understand the desired outcomes your clients prioritize in their own lives. Aligning your product features to the outcomes they seek is the essence of problem-solution fit, and the first step towards launching products your clients will love.

* * *

Mike Cappucci is a Partner at FoundationLab. A lawyer turned product designer, Mike and the FoundationLab team collaborate with legal organizations to drive innovation efforts and build scalable, productized legal services. He can be reached at mike@foundationlab.co.

When a productized service replaces tasks currently done by humans, you'll need a convincing reason why a client should use your productized version instead. Maybe you can do it more conveniently, maybe for a fraction of the cost, or maybe you're offering something in a tiny niche that attorneys local to them don't offer. Ultimately, there has to be a benefit over-and-above the current offering, and now is the time to develop a theory as to why. You'll test it later on to see if it is supported by evidence from people you interview.

One other niche that is especially attractive for productized services: the "latent" market. This is where people have an addressable legal problem, but there is no one currently offering it at a price they're willing or able to pay for it. There's some debate as to just how big the latent legal market is, but there seems to be general consensus that it's in the tens of *billions* of dollars. It could even be larger: Over $400 billion is spent every year on legal services in the United States, and it's estimated that more than three-quarters of addressable legal problems still go unresolved.[3]

In the next chapter, you'll take this idea about solving a specific problem for a specific user and check out the competitive environment. Having an understanding of how others have tried to address the challenge, including where they have failed and succeeded in doing so, will give you more information about how to position your project.

Exercise: How Might We

This exercise is intended to help you identify target users and to start to develop an idea for a solution you will create. This is an iterative process, so it may be that further research later suggests returning to this step and choosing a new pairing to test. For now, though, this exercise will give you the kernel of a project.

To do this exercise, follow these steps:

1. Start by thinking through who you have defined as your target users and the problem you perceive that they have. Then reformat that information a bit using the "how might we" format. Write out the following, inserting the appropriate information:

   How might we help [insert summary of target user] to [insert summary of problem] by using [insert a form of productization described in chapter 3]?

---

3. For a thoughtful discussion of this topic, read/listen to this interview with the CEO of Clio, Jack Newton: https://legaltalknetwork.com/podcasts/clio-matters/2020/02/why-the-latent-legal-market-matters/.

For example, your "how might we" statement might look like:

> How might we help Massachusetts residential real estate attorneys to save wasted time waiting at the registry by using checklists?

2. Now, repeat this at least three different times, but for each repetition, insert a different form of productization in the final blank (e.g., an app or a newsletter).

You will now have three separate "how might we" sentences written on a piece of paper. For each, generate three separate "answers" to the "how might we" sentence you have created. For example:

> How might we help Massachusetts residential real estate attorneys to save wasted time waiting at the registry by using checklists?
>
> - Option 1: We could create a checklist of work that can be done on a smartphone from outside the office while the attorney waits.
> - Option 2: We could create a checklist of items the attorney needs with her to get the papers filed so that she isn't sent to the back of the line.
> - Option 3: We could create a checklist of other matters the attorney might also have business on at the registry so that she doesn't waste trips.

After you've created your responses — three answers each to three separate "how might we" statements — select the *one* problem statement and the *one* accompanying option you consider the most promising. That will become your starting point for what to build. Finalize this step by writing, in bold text, your selected "how might we" statement and single-sentence solution on slide two of your pitch deck.

Chapter 6

Survey the Competitive Environment

I n this chapter, you'll learn about the value and process of researching and assessing the competition. But first, it's worth noting that not every luminary in the business world tips their hat at this time-honored practice. Some innovative thinkers have had enormous success in business because they deliberately ignored the competition; they chose instead to chart a course of their own, alone on the open sea.

CREATING UNIQUE PRODUCTS

Who doesn't love the circus? Dubious ethics of using elephants aside, it's pure fun. The reality, though, is that creating a circus of your own—no matter how passionate you might be about clowns, lion taming, or high wire acts—is a terrible idea. The market has been shrinking for decades, and even the Ringling Brothers folded after 150 years of creating memories. It's very expensive and also logistically challenging to maintain a circus. But something a little different could work. Take Cirque du Soleil, for example. While traditional circuses were benchmarking against other traditional circuses in an effort to appropriate popular acts and market share (within a shrinking demand pool), Cirque du Soleil got busy reinventing the whole business. First, they eliminated costly factors that did not add customer value. Customers did not require animals for their entertainment, so Cirque du Soleil eliminated animals from the program and proceeded to create a show that was entertaining for both children *and* adults by making productions that were theatrical and artistic as well as fun. By bringing more "Broadway" into their circus, they were even able to raise ticket prices, as if they were in the theater industry.

Cirque du Soleil is a prime example of the "Blue Ocean Strategy," a technique that encourages business owners to open new market spaces with no competition and to focus on being in a class of one.[1] In other words, forget about what has come before: Sail in a vast blue ocean, with no one else around.

As co-founder of PayPal and startup guru Peter Thiel—himself an adherent to a form of this strategy—put it, "Competition is for losers."[2] Instead of competing, the goal should be to create a one-off, a product in a category of its own. Instead of starting a business that will inevitably lead to fights over price and other factors with market leaders who are equally or more capable than your company of delivering the same or a very similar product, you should strive to avoid all that by focusin
g on being unique.

Don't ask, "What great business can I get into ... ?" As Thiel suggests, your question should be, "What great business is *nobody* building?"

Think Cirque du Soleil, not Ringling Brothers.

FINDING YOUR OWN SPACE

Let's say that you've read through the previous chapters, you've spent some time soul-searching to identify your goals and resources, and now you have one or two intriguing ideas for creating a productized service. The next step is to see whether those ideas already exist in the market, and if so, what to do about it.

This part of the process is similar to the work law students and law professors do when deciding whether to write a law review article on a given topic: They do a "preemption" search to see if their

---

1. This anecdote, and many other terrific ones, are told in a slightly different form in the 2004 book, *Blue Ocean Strategy* by W. Chan Kim and Renée Mauborgne (Boston: Harvard Business School Press, 2015). The book provides an entire framework for thinking about building businesses that will monopolize a market, not compete with others in it.

2. https://www.wsj.com/articles/peter-thiel-competition-is-for-losers-1410535536.

idea for a thesis has already been published. Sometimes, they find that their idea is totally novel. More often, they find that the existing scholarship thoroughly covers the entire field. Still other times, the idea has been tried in the past, but time and perspectives have changed enough that it's worth trying again using the lessons learned from past efforts. You just can't know whether it makes sense to pursue a new idea until you've asked what else has been done on it.

Analyzing your potential competition has a few benefits. It prevents you from putting resources into developing something that is already available. Beyond that, it gives you a better understanding of trends and tactics that are (or are not) working. And it gives you a tangible feel for how the potential competition looks, and how it is marketed. By doing a competitive analysis, you can confirm if your product idea is new. But even if it isn't unique, your efforts can yield important insights into how you might improve upon what others have done with the same or a similar concept. All of this information will enable you to create more solid business strategies.

While the language of competitive analysis is taken from the business world, the process should be followed the same way even for those planning on building a free tool or otherwise not looking to turn a profit. There are two reasons for this: First, even if you intend to give something away, it makes little sense to reinvent the effort others have taken to build another version of it. Second, many projects, even if they don't cost end users anything, still have a cost to maintain. If there's no realistic opportunity to earn revenue because a competitor already occupies the space, it might mean you should consider another plan (or reach out to others already working on the problem that matters to you and see how you might collaborate).

EXPERT INSIGHT FROM JARED CORREIA

Lawyers tend to look beyond the legal industry for inspiration at gunpoint only. But, the fact of the matter is that, when a law firm gets into the product game, it opens itself to competition from better-funded, multi-state corporations that don't need to abide by the same ethics rules that law firms do. So, if you want to build a legal product out of a law firm, you better understand your value proposition like the contours of your boxer shorts. And if you don't know why a local option, developed by a law firm, isn't more viable than what a corporation can develop and sell, and if you're not willing to lean into that proposition . . . then, don't even bother to get started.

* * *

Jared D. Correia, Esq., is a business management consultant for lawyers and has developed a chatbot service built for lawyers. He can be reached at jared@redcavelegal.com.

In a competitive analysis, you would complete the three steps laid out in the next sections.

1. Determine Who Your Competitors Are

There are fundamentally two types of competitors, direct and indirect.

- **Direct competitors** are productized services that could pass as similar enough substitute for yours and that operate in your same geographic area (to the extent geography is relevant to your product, that is).
- **Indirect competitors** are not the "same" but could satisfy the same customer need or solve the same problem. Include in this list businesses that are selling the thing you want to productize in the form of a service. For example, if you plan to create an online tool to help lawyers with their specific, niche tax needs, look to see not just whether any current apps or

websites do this (those would be "direct competitors"), but whether any CPAs or tax advisors in the area you want to service have this specialty.

When comparing your brand, *focus on direct competitors*. Now, this doesn't mean you should toss your indirect competitors out the window completely. Indirect competitors should still stay on your radar because their product offerings could develop over time and become direct competitors. Beyond that, indirect competitors offering the service version of your product are competitors in the sense that if you're going to pry customers from them that they're currently serving, you'll need to be able to demonstrate that you offer them a real benefit (e.g., lower cost, more convenient assistance, and so on).

2. Determine What Your Direct Competitors Offer

For each direct competitor,[3] ask yourself the following:

- What makes them unique?
- What are they charging for their services?
- What are the characteristics and needs of their ideal customers?
- How do your competitors differentiate themselves from their competitors?
- How do they distribute their products/services?

3. Perform a Simplified SWOT Analysis of Each Direct Competitor

In a SWOT analysis, you evaluate your competitor's strengths and weaknesses, as well as the opportunities for your idea and the threats to your idea that others might pose. Put succinctly, the idea is for you to find things you can do better than others and to recognize those you can't. For example, if you're creating a new self-help

---

3. For indirect competitors, consider what they do/offer that you might be able to capture in your new product. You should also ask how difficult it would be for indirect competitors you have identified to pivot and become direct competitors (and how you would differentiate yourself if they did so).

divorce app, you might recognize that you have a strength in being able to customize the materials to your specific jurisdiction and provide detailed guidance in a way no other app does. You might also recognize that you have specific expertise in that area of law, so that you can ask very focused questions. However, you might recognize a weakness in that doing complex calculations for a divorce is best done using existing spreadsheet software and no matter how much you invest in an app it will be unlikely to create financial documents as efficiently as Excel could.

Some questions to get you started on this assessment include:

- What is your competitor doing really well?
- What is the weakest area for your competitor?
- Where does your brand have the advantage over your competitor?
- In what areas would you consider this competitor a threat?

Through this process, you'll be able to compare the strengths and weaknesses of the competition against your own strengths and weaknesses. By doing this, you will focus on working to your unique strengths and abilities, as well as starting to uncover areas for improvement within your own project.

In addition, with a good sense of who else is out there, you can transition to the next step: thinking about communicating to others what you're planning to do and helping them to understand why they should buy into your vision. This chapter was designed to help you make sure that your approach presents a new story. The next chapter will give you a framework to start testing the narrative about what you are building and to get a sense of the response it will get from potential users.

Exercise: Competitive Analysis

Take the idea that you identified in the exercise in chapter 5 and its direct competitors.* For each one, write out the following:

1. The competitor's name and, if applicable, a URL
2. A one-sentence summary of what the competitor does.
3. Answer the SWOT analysis questions:
   a. What are your strengths when measured against your competitor?
   b. What are your weaknesses when measured against your competitor?
   c. What are areas in the market the competitor could exploit?
   d. What are the threats to this competitor's business?

*If there are no "direct competitors," do this process for the three closest indirect competitors.

Now, let's add to our portfolio. Much like courtroom advocacy, we want to focus our portfolio to accentuate the positive, so our efforts here can go from "objective" to "persuasive" in considering the competition. Our goal is to show supporters that you have done your homework to identify other entities working in the same space, and that you have a plan to beat them, head-to-head. To do so, for any direct competitor only (no need to list indirect competitors), add the following to slide 3:

1. Name of the direct competitor
2. What the competitor does (in one sentence)
3. What you will do to differentiate yourself from that competitor

If no competition exists, write on the slide that you have performed a competitive survey, and that your productized service idea is sailing in clear waters.

Chapter 7

Create and Test an Elevator Pitch

When I was a practicing litigator, one of my colleagues would spend her time in the days leading up to trials talking to anyone who would listen about the upcoming case. She had a very specific formula for doing so: She would leave the office to take a walk. During her walk, she would strike up a conversation with random people on the escalator, the security guards at the building's entrance, and anyone browsing at a nearby newspaper stand.

She'd say, "I'm a lawyer, and I've got a trial coming up. Can I get your thoughts in response to a few questions?"

In a minute flat, she'd describe the key details of the facts, say something about the parties to the case, and bring out the key arguments she anticipated. Plain language, straightforward. Then she'd ask a simple question.

"No holds barred—what do you think?"

Sometimes the person would tell her that her client sounded like a jerk. Sometimes, they'd say she had a million-dollar case.

She would do this over and over, always giving the key facts of the case and asking people—people just like the jurors deciding her case—what they thought about this or that aspect of the case.

Over time, she saw the power in this method of research. She came to see that when certain patterns emerged, it was a good sign; and when other patterns emerged, it was important to change something about her case. This practice of pitching a question or idea to someone on an elevator or at a newsstand is the basis of using "elevator pitches" in market research. It's a tried-and-true method for gleaning useful feedback from all sorts of people. And that sort of feedback is useful for all sorts of people—from writers with a script, to lawyers with a case, to entrepreneurs with an idea.

It will be part of your approach, too.

So far, this process has been about you and your best guess for what will make for a good productized service. It's great to build a product that solves *your* problem, but your product won't succeed unless you build something that solves problems for lots of other people, too. Now is the time to start talking to lots of other people about your idea to get useful feedback.

PRE-LAUNCH TESTS AND CHECK-INS

This will be a recurring theme: Before you launch any product, it's wise to go through a number of tests and check-ins to see if the increasingly heavy investment of your time, money, and other resources is likely to bear fruit.

Check in with people you have identified as experts and potential supporters in the area that you're building for. The goal is to gauge their response to discover if there's something big that you're missing or that should result in adopting a different approach to the project or pursuing a different project altogether. Making this check-in requires that you build a support network.

Building a support network around your *idea* is a different process from collecting *user* feedback based on a prototype of your idea. (The prototype comes later and is more involved.) Talking to your support network about your idea is similar to fielding your colleagues for their gut response to whether a case is viable or not. Testing reactions to a prototype is more like hiring a mock jury to test out your trial argument. (Same case, very different stages in its development.)

Creating a Support Network

Getting early reaction is only part of the reason to start pitching your idea. There are several advantages to reaching out to others early. First, it helps you focus on what you want to do by forcing you to create a succinct summary of what you plan to do and why you think it will matter. The process of creating the pitch and actually talking it through with live humans helps focus the concept. Second, the network provides a way to develop support. Finding people who are ready to offer their wisdom, money, and feedback will help throughout the project and will help you launch successfully. Third, building a network means building a group of potential loyal users. If you involve people from the demographic you imagine will ultimately make use of the product and then build it to incorporate their desires for how it should work, you've got a natural opening when it comes to actually selling them or others like them the product. Finally, having a network lets the world know that you are a creative force: You're building something, you're pushing the envelope, and you're looking for ways to improve yourself and your organization. Wearing this identity will pay dividends for this project, and potentially far beyond.

Engineering this support network need not be difficult, in large part because these are likely people you already know or who are in your larger orbit. For example, if you're building a tool to make the work of filing immigration court paperwork more efficient, you can ask colleagues in your firm's immigration department, contacts from the local immigration bar association, or people working in the area that you are connected with on LinkedIn or other social media sites. Asking for a few minutes of time to get insights about an idea you have—one that's relevant to a shared interest—typically gets a good response. If people say no, that's OK too: Just keep moving and reaching out.

In making these contacts, you'll want to seek out the people who would use your product: the end users who represent the market for your product. If your product is fully realized, you'll be selling it to them. That's why it's important to ask them for input at the outset.

Your Elevator Pitch

A terrific technique for gauging someone's response to you and your idea is to boil down to 60 seconds who you are and what your idea is.

This is called an "elevator pitch," and its purpose is to explain your concept quickly, clearly, and in a way that sparks interest in who you are and what you do. It should be short enough to get your message across anytime and anywhere—even during a quick ride on an elevator.

You'll have a natural tendency to want to say *everything* about your idea—don't. Be brief. A good elevator pitch must be so compelling that, once you've finished, whoever you're talking to will be interested enough to support your project.

QUESTIONS TO KEEP IN MIND WHEN CREATING AN ELEVATOR PITCH

When developing your elevator pitch, consider the following questions:

1. Who Are You?

If the person you're pitching isn't someone you're close to, summarize in a sentence who you are and what you do. For example:

> *"I'm a law professor who teaches people to navigate the intersection of law, innovation, technology, and entrepreneurship."*

2. What Do You Do or Offer?

Add a sentence or two about what you do every day in your business. For example:

> *"In class, I teach students a process for turning work done repeatedly into work that can be done automatically with expanded reach. This allows them to deliver better value to their clients and make more money for themselves."*

3. What Problem Do You Solve?

Identify the value you intend to offer with your productized service to your target users. For example:

"Outside of my in-person classes, there aren't any easy avenues for students at other schools or for legal professionals to learn these methods. I want to boil these concepts down into a how-to book that takes people through the process of developing their own productized service to fill that gap."

4. How Are You Different?

Tell the person you are pitching what sets you apart from others. Whether you're the first to do something, uniquely positioned because of your unique experience, or otherwise have a special ability to share the information, it's important to get that across. This is your core narrative. For example:

"No one else has created a 'how-to' book on this topic. Because of my experience teaching it in the classroom and helping law firms and other organizations through this process, I have the ability to share my perspective and help people learn this set of skills."

5. Ask a Question

Elevator pitches are generally delivered in person, which means you want to be social and engage your lead in a conversation. A great way to involve your lead is to ask a question that relates to your lead and your business. For example:

"What is your firm/organization doing about getting people to think about creating products that will benefit your clients and make you more profitable?"

6. Give a Call to Action

Once your pitch is done, give the lead something to do. Briefly let your audience know what they can do to follow up and hear more. Provide a means for further contact or for scheduling a meeting. For example:

"One of the things that's important to me is involving industry experts so I can shape this project to make sure it's as useful as

it can be. First, I'd love to have your reaction to this idea, and second, if you're interested, I'd be pleased to send you over the chapters I've drafted and give you a preview. If you have ideas after you've checked it out, I'd love to incorporate them."

The Goal of the Elevator Pitch

The primary goal of an elevator pitch is to gauge how well your idea is received. Optimally, your audience will declare it the best idea they've ever heard and pledge their ongoing support and loyalty, explaining why it's so valuable to them. A "good" alternative outcome is that they furrow their brow and say, "Sounds interesting, but what about X?" and sink your idea altogether. Remember, at this point, we're still in an early phase of testing this hypothesis, so hearing early on that the idea might encounter problems you haven't anticipated is a good outcome in the sense that it lets you reset the process before you've gotten too deeply involved.

WHAT TO DO WITH WHAT YOU LEARN

Just because a person responds positively to your idea doesn't mean that it's going to be a runaway success. Liking an idea and being willing to lend support to an idea (or even pay for an idea) are vastly different things. Often, a person will want to support *you* and so will be supportive of an idea that, if offered by someone else, might not be one they would get behind. Ultimately, what you're looking for is a pattern of positive feedback. That should be cause for encouragement, but you still have a long way to go.

On the flip side, you should also not be deflated if someone offers negative feedback. Just because an idea doesn't speak to one person, doesn't mean it is a bad idea. It's simply not for *them*. One reason to pitch the idea to several people is that you're looking for patterns. If every person you pitch thinks the idea is bad, and can articulate reasons why, it's important to take a step back and consider their answers. Perhaps you can use that information to adapt your idea and then re-pitch in its new formulation. Or perhaps, there's good reason the project won't work, and your contacts' feedback makes you realize how and why. In that case, back up a few steps and try something new!

* * *

Now that you've gotten a sense of how your idea is received condensed into an elevator pitch, it's time to actually move toward making a tangible thing. Words only have so much oomph: In the next chapter, you'll take the initial responses you've received from others and start shaping what you've learned from them into a prototype that allows for deeper engagement with your users.

Exercise: The Elevator Pitch

Create an elevator pitch for your project. Start by writing it out and then practice it enough times that you are ready to try it verbally.

Next, find at least three people you consider respected mentors, peers, or potential supporters of your project. Pop into their office or find them at the next organizational cocktail party and ask for a moment of their time to run an idea past them, and do your pitch.

After the event, write down how they responded, what feedback they offered, and whether they were interested in an opportunity to follow up on the idea. From there, look for patterns in the information you have gathered from these pitches. If you were to create a one- or two-sentence summary of what people said, what would it be? What about a one-sentence summary of the positive responses? The negative responses?

For those who wanted to learn more, set up a time to discuss your project in more detail, and keep them involved!

Chapter 8

Create a Prototype

I f you ever find yourself in Florence, Italy, and on a tight schedule, I recommend you *not* go to the Galleria dell'Accademia di Firenze to see Michelangelo's *David*. Of course, Michelangelo's *David* is a masterpiece. Of course, seeing it would be memorable. The problem is, there are hundreds—if not thousands—of other amazing sights to see in Florence and seeing the *David* on a sweltering hot day in August can cost you four sweaty hours in line just to step foot inside the museum.

Instead, here's my recommendation: Head over to the Piazza della Signoria. It's the central location in the history of the Florentine Republic and a focal point of the city. It is where actual Florentines congregate, and a jumping-off point for several worthwhile tourist spots that don't have four-hour lines, including the Palazzo Vecchio, Piazza del Duomo, and the gateway to the Galleria degli Uffizi.

Piazza della Signoria also features an exact replica of Michelangelo's *David*! The Piazza della Signoria was, in fact, where the original *David* stood until 1910, when he was put behind walls at the Galleria dell'Accademia.

By going to the Piazza della Signoria to see the replica of *David* instead of the Galleria dell'Accademia, you'll get the fundamental experience of seeing David without the inconvenience involved in viewing the original. Really, unless you're well into your MFA degree in sculpture, you've got nothing to lose by choosing to see David's clone, except the opportunity to develop a heat rash from standing in line in the sun.

And this is how a good prototype works: It gives the idea of the full version and conveys the essence of what you want to share, but it skips the full version's inconvenient aspects.

This chapter looks at the goals behind creating a prototype and presents some of the essential tools and key steps that apply to developing a prototype for a productized service. Ultimately, you'll learn a method for capturing the most important features of the completed product you hope to create, but without spending a lot of time on the spit-and-polish features that take time to make without adding much value to the problem you're solving.

*   *   *

An essential step in creating something new is taking an early pass at it by creating a dynamic, realistic version that you could envision launching into the world. It's important to take time with this step for several reasons, but don't worry: Creating a prototype can be very fun, so it might not feel like "work."

The "look" of your prototype will depend on the service you intend to productize. For example, if you're creating an app (or otherwise creating a software-based product), your prototyping will take a different form than if your product is a newsletter. The app might just be a mock-up on PowerPoint, where clicking a "button" on the app will advance to the next slide, simulating the next screen on the app. The newsletter could be a simple Word document laid out to look like a newsletter. Either way, you should follow the prototyping process: Creating a mock-up for something printed will yield valuable insights, just as mocking up a piece of software will.

GOALS OF PROTOTYPING

There are three core reasons that you need to create a prototype.

1. Building a Prototype Helps You Hone Your Idea

Ideas always work well inside your own head. It's when you go to execute an idea that the challenges and flaws you didn't see on your own bubble up. You'll never be aware of these issues unless you build a test version and give it a ride.

2. You'll Need a Prototype to Demonstrate to Target Users How Your Productized Service Works

In the next chapter, you'll be asked to show potential end users the product you are building and get their guidance about what is—and is not—working. This prototype is what you will show them. Your audience may need to use some level of imagination to envision the final product, but the prototype will at least put them in the correct mindset to respond to it.

3. It Will Encourage Others to Take You More Seriously

When you arrive for user interviews (more on that in the next chapter!) or in your boss's office to ask for financial support to bring an idea to life, having a prototype shows that the idea is more than a concept in your head. It's a tangible, visible thing, and that gives weight to your project. Talk is cheap—but prototypes demonstrate action.

EXPERT INSIGHT FROM JARED CORREIA

The first step that software companies take beyond planning is to create what's called an "MVP," or minimal viable product. In other words, those companies ask themselves: "What's the baseline product I can offer to the public without completely destroying my credibility?" Part of the reason that businesses apply this strategy is so that their products don't end up in development hell—because at some point, the product has got to be released, and it's not going to be perfect. The company must iterate on its offering to continue to improve; and real feedback only comes about when you release your idea into the wild. Law firms are generally uncomfortable with that model; generally speaking, attorneys hold onto their work product like a tiny baby bird with brittle bones. If you want to sell law firm products, though, you're going to need to get comfortable with experimentation.

* * *

Jared D. Correia, Esq., is a business management consultant for lawyers and has developed a chatbot service built for lawyers. He can be reached at jared@redcavelegal.com.

HOW TO PROTOTYPE

There's no one-size-fits-all form of prototyping simply because there are so many different types of productized services. Your overarching goal will be to create a single prototype that represents what you hope your final product will look like so that you can show it to end users and get their feedback on it. The prototype can include only one small part of the envisioned product. It can be a simplified version. But it has to give the flavor of the ultimate product. One example is providing a single chapter plus a table of contents for a proposed manual covering processes for handling an immigration matter. The aim is to make a prototype as true to your envisioned final version as possible without putting undue time or money into producing it.

Here are some additional examples of relatively straightforward prototypes:

- If you're creating a newsletter, a prototype issue of the newsletter could include the sorts of links, narratives, and headings that you plan to include in the real thing.
- For a training manual, a sample chapter, together with a table of contents, may be all you need for a successful prototype.
- A suite of automated documents that allow users to defend a lawsuit could be prototyped using a single, automated legal form that demonstrates what the overall package and its user interface will look like.
- If you are prototyping a calculator, an image of what the app will look like, with the formula prototyped in Excel, would serve your purposes.

Productizing Complex Products

As productized services become more complex, prototyping becomes more challenging. Take, for example, a multi-page website that serves as a client portal. In that example, you might need to take shortcuts by providing prototypes of only a few of the pages most representative of the final project. There is nothing wrong with taking that approach when prototyping a product.

Ultimately, the goal is for the prototype to be as close a representation of what you envision for the final version as possible. This will have the benefit of reducing wasted resources if you validate your idea and create a final version. It also will prevent enthusiastic potential early adopters to whom you show the prototype from being disappointed or confused if the final version looks different.

Making a Hand-Drawn Prototype

Even a very complex app can be modeled well enough using a pencil and paper to get useful feedback. The goal is to create as accurate a representation as possible as to how the tools will look and behave when users interact with them. As a preliminary step (or if you're not comfortable using wireframing software, discussed later in this chapter), you can just use a pencil.

You'll need to get the right tools: a pencil, an eraser, and paper. It helps to have a web-enabled computer, printer, and photocopier, too. This allows you to do a web search to find templates showing blank versions of the final form of your product. For example, if you envision your creation as an iPhone app, go online and do an image search for "blank iPhone screen template." Voilà, you'll get dozens of hits for blank templates that allow you to print something that approximates the dimensions of a blank iPhone screen. (Of course, if your product is paper-based, like a manual, there's no need to search far; it's just a matter of formatting a Word document to approximate how you plan your manual will look.) Print out several of the templates. Now, draw what you want the landing page to look like when someone first arrives on your app. Include the relevant boxes, buttons, and text.

Give your user the experience you expect them to have on the app, even if it's in paper form and drawn with pencil. Be as accurate with the form as you want it to be when it becomes a reality. To the extent anything on the screen requires explanation, you can annotate it with a blurb outside the template. However, part of the challenge of building apps, websites, and tech tools is that they basically have to speak for themselves. So if you don't think people will understand your creation without annotations, take the time to revise the prototype until they will.

If the front page of your site or app asks users to click buttons, draw follow-up pages showing what the subsequent pages will look like. As with the landing page, include all relevant text, images, and buttons. Repeat the process for each subpage you envision. When drawing subpages, decide at the outset if you want to have a consistent theme to your template, such as the name of the app at the top of the page, or a sidebar that lists various forms available. If so, draw that basic theme onto the template and then make several photocopies so that you need not repeat the process of making the theme for each subpage.

Ultimately, once you've drawn pictures of all the relevant screens, put them in a stack. When you're doing your interviews, you'll ask the person you're interviewing to interact with the pages as if they were an actual app. You'll ask them to push the drawn-in "buttons" on the paper screen. When they do, you will flip to the relevant subpage representing where the pressed button would take them. To make sure you have drawn a page for every relevant screen, try to envision every combination of buttons the interview subject might press and make sure there is a subpage picture for each of them.

This will be a good starting place, particularly if you've got a product idea that is fairly straightforward and can be demonstrated with a few simple pictures. In some instances, you'll need to go beyond this.

Multiple Prototypes

Some creators have two competing ideas about the best way to make their project look or behave. If this is your situation, prototype both versions. The process of modeling both may reveal to you why one is better than the other. If not, bring both versions to your interview sessions (discussed in the next chapter) and get feedback on both before deciding which way to go.

Using Software to Prototype

If you're comfortable using it, all of the processes described for paper prototyping can be done using software, and generally the resulting prototype will look more polished. The web has no shortage of free "wireframing" tools, which are low-fidelity, basic layout and structural guidelines of a web product's layout; prototypes use advanced wireframes with more visual detail and interaction options. Wireframes can make prototypes that include working buttons, links to subpages that "feel" like a working website, and more. They are relatively inexpensive, and easy to learn.

One can also create prototypes using existing tools that many will be familiar with. For example, you can make a prototype of an app or website using demonstration software (like PowerPoint, Keynote, or Google Slides). These prototypes will be easy to make for those who have general familiarity with these tools (and if you're not familiar with them, you can do a quick search for "prototyping using [insert name of software]" and find plenty of tutorials). You can get started by doing a web search for "making prototypes using PowerPoint" (or whatever presentation software you prefer). There are several easy tutorial videos online that can demonstrate the process in just a few minutes.

A new generation of "no-code" tools are also available that enable non-techies to create beautiful prototypes that are also sophisticated finished products. These tools enable a complete novice to create perfectly good low-tech products, like eBooks and email newsletters, or far more sophisticated projects, like expert systems and document assembly tools.

Before drawing a paper prototype, spend some time searching to see if a no-code tool is out there that suits your needs. It may be enough to create a prototype, if nothing else. If you're lucky, a no-code tool exists that will allow you to create your finished product. If so, you should certainly spend a few minutes getting familiar with it and create the prototype using it.

DOCUMENT ASSEMBLY AS AN OPPORTUNITY FOR CLIENT COLLABORATION

Document automation has historically been used for internal document drafting. But with online portals and paywall capabilities, many lawyers are using Documate to collaborate with their clients and provide subscription-based services. Two examples of law firms who have turned their expertise into sophisticated subscription legal products are LCN Legal and Freshlease.

LCN Legal is a law firm with offices in the UK and China. It specializes in corporate structures for multinational groups, and acts for clients globally, specifically as a leader in the legal implementation of transfer pricing compliance through intercompany agreements. LCN Legal determined that some of its work, while incredibly complex, could be turned into legal workflows if enough thought went into the process of developing the software. Consequently they built several expert systems using Documate to enable non-lawyers to produce best-in-class intercompany agreements, as well as suites of documents for implementing certain types of domestic corporate structures and reorganization projects. The firm makes its document automation tools available to third parties, both on a pay-per-use and on a subscription basis. Alongside the subscription, it also offers various other online/digital products, including an online course in intercompany agreements and toolkits of template intercompany agreements (sold on a subscription basis).

Similarly, the law firm Strang Parish & Graham released a legal technology product called FreshLease (www .freshlease.com). FreshLease is an expert system that helps landlords create professional, up-to-date leases anytime, anywhere. Strang Parish & Graham's sophisticated residential lease generator is constantly updated to meet the ever-changing state of the law and best practices. Their clients constantly access the software to generate new leases, so they give landlords unlimited access to the platform through a subscription model.

* * *

Dorna Moini is the founder of Documate, a no-code platform for creating legal products. Prior to founding Documate she was a litigator, and she currently teaches the Legal Innovations Lab at USC Law School. She can be reached at dorna@documate.org.

Outsourcing Prototyping

If you have a budget and don't relish the idea of learning how to use wireframe software, there is also no shortage of companies and consultants who specialize in creating prototypes for clients. Some even specialize in helping clients in the legal industry. This approach will be more efficient and reduce the process fits-and-starts arising when busy people are learning unfamiliar skills.

However, outsourcing can be problematic, too. Building your own prototype makes you the ultimate tester in some senses. You'll have to think through the logic, fix mistakes or illogical sequences, and wrestle with the best way to share your idea. Beyond that, part of the joy of creating a product is that it can be a "homegrown" accomplishment, and you shouldn't overlook the psychological cost of outsourcing *your* process of creation.

* * *

Now that you've built something that embodies your idea (and started to gather some evidence that it's got a place in the market based on your research and the feedback from elevator pitches), you can move forward with a real, tangible *thing* to show off. In the next chapter, you'll learn how to interview others using your prototype and to make changes to your plan based on what you learn.

Exercise: Make a Prototype

Follow the instructions from this chapter and make a prototype. Once you have done so, create a slide showing the main page and any other page(s) you consider key to your productized service (if you chose to make a paper prototype, make a scan of it).

After you have interviewed users and updated the prototype, you will update the slide to show the changes you have made in response to user feedback.

Chapter 9

Seek End-User Feedback— And Iterate Based on It

L EGO has been producing their interlocking bricks since the 1940s. Today, LEGO is worth several billion dollars in sales annually. Their toys are so popular that there are an estimated 62 LEGO blocks for every single human on earth today.[1] And they no longer make just bricks; their product line extends to retail stores, a theme park, and LEGO movies. And when it comes to the traditional LEGO brick, they don't just sell them in generic packs. LEGO packages their bricks (of various shapes and colors) as part of a wide array of themed *sets*, which kids and kids-at-heart can use to build LEGO pirate ships, LEGO Star Wars characters, LEGO Harry Potter scenes, and LEGO etcetera, etcetera.

But it's *how* LEGO develops their packaging ideas that interests us: They ask their customers.

The LEGO Ideas website invites customers to submit their product ideas. Anyone can build a model using their own bricks and post what they envision as a new, original LEGO set that LEGO could sell. Through a guided process, other LEGO enthusiasts are encouraged to review these proposed new models and become "supporters" for the models they like. When enough people support a new model concept, LEGO's staff will review it. If the LEGO staff believe that there's a market for it, they will develop that idea as a new product to market and sell.

With the LEGO Ideas website, not only does LEGO receive great ideas, LEGO has also created a process for discovering whether an

---

1. https://mashable.com/2014/09/11/5-facts-lego/?utm_source=feedly&utm_medium=webfeeds#rG9hk7blnZqK.

idea will sell to people who are passionate enough to spend time viewing other people's LEGO creations and evaluating them (for free).

Moreover, this same website builds community among LEGO fans because it gives them a chance to inspire one another and allows them to feel "heard" by the company.

All of this exemplifies how seeking user feedback can create a positive feedback loop.

*   *   *

You have an idea, you've done your research, you've sought input from respected mentors and peers, and you've built a model of it.

Now, it's time to test out your idea. This chapter lays out a process for testing your idea and gathering useful feedback from your target users. You'll also learn how to process and make the best use of the feedback you receive.

IDENTIFY YOUR INTERVIEW SUBJECTS

Who should you seek out to provide feedback? The people you want to weigh in on whether your idea will succeed, fail, or requires further development are your *intended target users*. In chapter 4, we discussed who your target users are in relation to your productized service.

How Do You Find Your End Users?

Rather than ask people you know well, you should look for connections and referrals from your personal network, colleagues, classmates, and sites like LinkedIn. You want objective feedback, so avoid interviewing anyone with whom you have a deep personal relationship. Reviewers should be drawn from as diverse a group as possible (e.g., people of various experience levels, ages, life experiences, and so on) within your target user community. The key, though, is that the interview subjects should be people you ultimately envision using the creation.[2]

---

2. There's an interesting question about getting feedback from customers vs. end users. A managing partner who makes the decision to purchase automation

You should plan to interview five people from your target group. This number is optimal because anything smaller will not provide enough data, while anything larger provides diminishing returns in terms of how much new ground they will break.[3]

The "ask" can be simple and straightforward: Contact potential interviewees and tell them you are working on a project that does X; you think they might someday benefit from it, and you would like to share your idea and ask their feedback and advice. Let them know that the conversation will only take a few minutes (30 minutes will do) and that you'll be glad to meet them somewhere or come to their office, whichever is convenient.[4] While opinions vary, I think it also makes sense to let them know that you are not trying to sell them anything (some people are gun-shy about participating in this sort of interview, because they envision it turning into a request for them to buy something or fund your project). Tell them straight out that you want to do this because you value their perspective, and you're going to ask for nothing except their time and feedback.

HOW THE TEAM BEHIND CLOSING FOLDERS USED EARLY FEEDBACK TO IMPROVE THEIR PRODUCT

I've talked about our legaltech product, Closing Folders, to many lawyers over the years. Telling the same story over and over again to so many different people has taught me a lot

---

software is the "customer" in that it is the managing partner who decides to purchase access; a paralegal using the software is the one end user in that they are, well, the person using it day to day. This is relevant because when you interview an end user about a product idea, their perspective is likely different than that of a person who won't be expected to use it regularly, but who does need to budget for it. For our purposes, the better goal is to interview end users while keeping in mind that if your idea is to be adopted, it will have to appeal to the interests of the customer, too!

3. I learned that this is the optimal number of interview subjects from the work of Jake Knaap. Knaap's book, *Sprint: How to Solve Big Problems and Test New Ideas in Just Five Days* (New York: Simon and Schuster, 2016), is an excellent, deep dive into the design sprint process.

4. Some people offer to pay interview subjects for their time. My experience is that this isn't necessary, as most people are happy to give a few minutes of their time to share their thoughts. If you think it necessary to offer some form of remuneration, you can offer early or free access to your product as a show of appreciation.

about patterns of behavior and helped me spot the discussions which have the most potential to be fruitful.

In the early days, I think the interview process has two purposes: (1) learning more about the problem you are trying to solve, and (2) recruiting your "first user."

For the first goal, every interview you conduct adds a new perspective to your understanding of the problem. However, if you pay too much attention to the averages of the feedback you receive, you are very likely to end up with a product that is liked by all, but loved by none. For this reason, I would recommend formulating your own thesis about what the product should be that discounts the opinions expressed in some of your interviews heavily and doubles down on others.

This is where the second goal, recruiting your "first user," comes into play. Through the interview process, you are really searching for one or two interactions where the interviewee really sees your vision and is prepared to buy into it. When you find that "first user," you'll want to go all in on making her fall in love with your product to the exclusion of everyone else you interview. If the candidate is right, this person will be willing to use the earliest, buggiest prototype of your product because she feels the pain it solves so acutely. If a "first user" never comes along despite many interviews, it might be a hint that the pain you are trying to solve is not felt strongly enough by your target customers to merit a stand-alone product.

I'm not sure exactly what a perfect "first user" interview looks like, but I know a few things it's not. One person who is definitely not your "first user" is the "yes man" who does not raise a single problem with your idea and only offers generic praise and encouragement. In my experience, these kinds of conversations seem encouraging at first, but on reflection you can see a lack of engagement with the questions and a tacit refusal to go deeper into the conversation with you. As it turns out, being extremely encouraging and agreeable is a great way for a lawyer to wrap up a conversation and move on to the next thing in his busy schedule. We were victim to this a bit but, as time went on, we learned to always ask more from these types of interviews until the interviewee is forced to reveal that they really aren't that interested (asking for money is a great way to do this!).

Another person who is not your "first user" is the "issue spotter." This person listens intently to your idea while actively looking to point out its weaknesses and problems. It can seem like they are engaging with your idea, but really, they are looking for an out so they can pass on the concept while making it appear that their resistance is the fault of your product. Every question you answer will be met with another objection until the issue spotter finally hits upon something to hang his hat on and kindly sees you to the door. It's tempting to come away from these discussions thinking that if you solved the issue spotter's final objection, he would be a user, but with an issue spotter there will always be another objection around the corner.

At one point early on at Closing Folders, a lawyer tried the product out for an afternoon and sent us a two-page, single-spaced list of problems with the software. We were eager to please, so we worked through the list for the next 48 hours until every problem had been addressed. That lawyer never tried the software again. To contrast that, one of our earliest users tried the product over the course of a month and ran an entire transaction on it. I went and sat with him in his office and asked how it went and he said, "It actually went pretty smoothly. I just wish I could see more closing items on the screen at once." It turns out we had designed our user interface with item titles that were three or four words long. In reality, the titles of his closing items were sometimes multiple paragraphs long. For a month he had been tediously scrolling up and down the page to view his closing agenda — something we could easily fix with a few small layout tweaks.

Once you've found your "first users" you'll want to invest heavily in your personal relationships with them and constantly return to them to review your latest ideas and prototypes. Your ultimate goal should be to get them using your product for real work as early as possible. Make sure to always be appreciative of their time investment and find ways to be generous in return. Once you have a few early users who really love what you are building so far, you can start to think about how to grow the feature set to get the next few. One of the few advantages of starting a new product is you can afford to invest almost limitless time in making your users happy.

*   *   *

Gordon Cassie is the cofounder of Closing Folders, a pioneer and leader in legal transaction management software. Previously, Gordon practiced law at a boutique corporate securities firm in Toronto.

Make a Short Presentation, Then Use the "I Like/I Wish/ What If" Format

First, even though you're preparing to do what we're calling an interview, don't think of it as a job interview or an academic interview. It's less a back-and-forth than it is you framing the conversation around discovering what your end user thinks about your prototype.

Okay, you've got your interview subject lined up. They are waiting in your office, and you have 30 minutes to present your prototype and chat.

Now what?

Pitch Your Idea

After greeting your interview subject, start by giving your elevator pitch—summarize in just a few seconds what your idea is and what it does. There is no need to follow a script, but it's useful to have an outline or checklist, so you can make sure you cover the big-ticket items you want to ask your subject about.

Present the Prototype

Then, put the prototype in front of them. Let them know that the buttons don't really work, but by some tech magic, they can see a sort of mirage of the idea you envision (if it's a paper prototype, have them tell you what button they'd press, and flip to that page).

Ask Open-Ended Questions

Once they have had a chance to play with the prototype, begin by asking questions. The key is to ask open-ended and follow-up questions that encourage your subject to flesh out *their* views.

- "I heard you say the layout is a little busy. What about how it looks don't you love?"
- "Can you say more about why you like the concept?"
- "You had some interesting ideas about adding more content. Where would you put it on the page?"

If they like something or don't like it, ask them, "Why?"

You can use the "I Like, I Wish, What if" format, which helps frame the discussion in a constructive, positive way, to get your subject talking.

In "I Like . . ." statements, the user is encouraged to convey the aspects that he or she liked about the prototype. This provides you with positive feedback about your prototype.

- "What do you like about what you've seen?"

In "I Wish . . ." statements, users are prompted to share ideas of how the prototype can be changed or improved to address some concerns or issues. This is an avenue to collect negative feedback and constructive criticism.

- "What do you wish was different about what you've seen?"

"What if . . ." questions encourage your subject to offer additional suggestions that might not have a direct link to your prototype, ideas that you may want to explore in future iterations of prototypes.

- "What suggestions do you have about what you've seen?"

Don't get stuck on the points of your outline or checklist; if your subject says something you want to dig into more deeply, just go for it. Ask follow-up questions. See where it leads.

The interview can be a good opportunity to pull out alternative prototypes you may have created earlier—to get feedback on them independently or to compare and contrast with the later prototype.

Be Open to Criticism

If you intended a feature of your product to do one thing, but your subject envisions it doing something else, your mission is to understand *why* they see it differently from you, not to correct their misapprehension.

Capture and Preserve Feedback

As your interview subject speaks, be sure to write down the main points of their comments. This is important information that you won't want to lose or forget.

Recording can change the tenor of the conversation, and if you're concerned about getting things down correctly, you can ask your interview subject if you can email your notes later, to make sure that you got it right. By and large, you should only write short phrases or points of significance that you have to remember, so handwriting will be sufficient.

Leave the Door Open for a Return Visit

As the interview winds down, thank the interview subject for their time, invite them to share any more feedback they think of, and then ask if you can follow up with them. From here, the process will involve making changes to your plan based on patterns of feedback you receive. Having the ability to circle back around to others who have seen earlier versions can be valuable. For that reason, ask to keep the door open.

THE POST-INTERVIEW PROCESS

Now that you've gathered all of these ideas, comments, and feedback from five different potential end users, what do you do with it all? The post-interview process boils down to two components: (1) analyzing the data you've gathered, and (2) developing a plan for revising.

Analyze Feedback and Look for Patterns

Once you've done all five interviews, it's time to analyze your feedback:

1. To start, divide a piece of paper into three columns (this will also work with sticky notes on a white board divided into thirds). At the top of the first column, write "I like"; at the top of the second, "I wish"; and at the top of the third, "What if."
2. Next, consolidate the feedback you've received from each interview subject into a single sentence for each column: If you interviewed five people, there will be five "I like" sentences, five "I wish" sentences, and five "What if" sentences. From there, paste/post that feedback into the appropriate column, so that you're left looking at all of the "I likes," "I wishes," and "What ifs" stacked on top of one another.
3. From here, take a look at the feedback you've received as a group. What patterns emerge? Are people offering the same advice, or appreciating the same features?

Consider Making Revisions Based on Patterns of Feedback

When you spot patterns of feedback (i.e., multiple people comment on a given point in a similar way), it's important to respond to them. This is rather straightforward in principle: If people really like a given feature, leave it be. If negative consensus emerges about an aspect of your prototype, think about how you could redesign or reimagine that part in keeping with the advice you've received. (Of course, this is still *your* productized service.) As you review the feedback, remember that this isn't a *quantitative* analysis—you're not just trying to assign scores to the points brought up and how often. Our goal is *qualitative*: We want to explore our interview subjects' ideas, attitudes, and experiences toward the product.

Sometimes, patterns of feedback will suggest that the interviewees have little interest in your product: Perhaps there's a competitor you didn't identify, or you misread the buzz about what you've made. In that case, it's important to take a step back and ask yourself:

- Do I need to reboot my process altogether?
- Could I develop one of the features of my product into *the* product?
- Could I take some other, third course, like greatly expanding a feature of the product?

Whichever way you ultimately go, your mindset should be, *I am not going to give up easily.* If the advice you've received is anathema to your vision or plan, that doesn't mean you should abandon your own good sense. The ultimate data point is going to be whether people adopt and use your build.

But you should remain open to testing out new ideas, to see if one or more could gain a better foothold with your target users. Your initial feedback could have been disappointing for any of several reasons: It could be that a paper prototype didn't test well when compared to a final, digital version. Maybe you had bad luck finding the right subjects to interview. Nonetheless, patterns matter, and they shouldn't be dismissed out of hand. You should at least consider making changes when your target audience recommends them.

A harder problem arises when the pattern of feedback is neutral or disjointed. When you look at the corpus of what you have learned, you'll need to do an honest assessment. If people are not excited about your product, it's a bad sign for its future. If they seem more confused than apathetic, then it's an opportunity to take a step back and decide if your prototype or interview approach needs to be revised. If, after a second pass, they still seem confused by it, take this as a major red flag. You can't sell what people don't like or don't understand. If you're not able to get a friendly audience excited about the concept, it likely will not become a productized service that has that impact.

A final caveat: Interview subjects tend to give rosier feedback when they have nothing to lose, compared to when a decision is required to purchase and use the product (or not). Recognize this phenomenon, and, if anything, hold on to a little skepticism in these earlier stages of market research — even if your target users all seem to be saying, "This is terrific, I can't wait to buy this!"

You'll discover whether they truly mean it only after you've launched your product and those early supporters become active users of what you've built.

HOW MYPADILLA.COM USES FEEDBACK TO IMPROVE THEIR PRODUCTIZED SERVICE

At the beginning, we leveraged connections with criminal attorneys, offering free advice in exchange for feedback on MyPadilla.com. We watched attorneys use an early version of the site with their clients, literally standing over their shoulders and observing how they interacted with it. Some things we thought were obvious turned out not to be obvious to all users. Other features were being misused. We learned a great deal from this process, which resulted in us creating a long list of modifications to make to improve the user experience. We've also used comprehensive surveys to dig into why attorneys have, and have not, adopted the tool. This has allowed us to better hone the offering to make it useful to our community.

I've come to realize that what makes a person a great lawyer can make them a really bad product developer. Lawyers want full information before acting, and want to avoid risks whenever possible. Being willing to try experiments and take some risks are at the core of developing a new product.

* * *

> *Julie Wimmer is a Texas-based immigration attorney and the founder of MyPadilla.com. Her productized service connects criminal defense attorneys with expertise on the collateral impact of guilty pleas in criminal cases on clients' immigration status. She can be reached at julie@mypadilla.com.*

Each stage of this process requires putting more "skin in the game" as you develop your product. This is with good cause, because each step provides support for the idea that you have a potentially successful idea (or giving the necessary feedback to help you recognize that you don't). Putting real skin in the game comes soon, though, in the form of money. If your responses have been positive to this point, it's time to start thinking about how you'll get your idea off the ground, and the next chapter helps to frame a business case to do so.

Exercise: Interview End-Users and Analyze the Patterns of Feedback

Interview 5 people using the method laid out in this chapter and write a one-page summary about the patterns you identified in their responses and what actions you will take to address that information.

Chapter 10

Build a Business Case

F or more than a decade, the ABC reality show *Shark Tank* has captivated viewers. It features a panel of investors, the "sharks," who decide whether or not to invest in a company or product based on the presentations of aspiring entrepreneurs. The sharks can spot weaknesses and faults in the entrepreneurs' valuation of their company, product, or business model—and typically decline to invest. But, occasionally, they are so impressed with the people, concept, and presentation that they will invest their own money in the project.

The ability of entrepreneurs to convince a shark that their idea, team, and business are worth investing in is an important skill—one that leads to dramatic moments on TV, and in real life, too.

WHAT IS A BUSINESS CASE AND WHY DO YOU NEED ONE?

In most new business ventures, a new product can only get off the ground with adequate outside support. That support could take the form of investors whose money allows you to hire coders or create a website. Or it could be a boss who is willing to give you a day or a week to develop this project as part of your normal schedule. Even if you never appear on *Shark Tank*, to keep your project moving forward you will need to persuade people that it is in their best interest to invest time, money, or labor into your project.[1]

You need to make a case for your project: a *business case*.

---

1. Unfortunately, this is true even if you're building a product for the common good: Developers might offer a discount to build your legal aid app, but they need to eat, too (though there are sometimes grants and often generous discounts from

Presenting Your Business Case

Your job in sharing a business plan is to gain support for your idea from those who will give you resources to do it—whether their time or money or other means. Thousands of successful entrepreneurs have done this and have passed on advice about the information you should expect to provide. This section lays out that advice.

The Traditional Business Plan

Traditionally, new companies draft business plans for three specific reasons: to articulate their vision for the business, to document how they plan to solve key challenges, and to pitch their business idea to potential investors.[2] However, some view these to be unnecessary because they are time-consuming to prepare, quickly become outdated, and go unread by busy prospective investors and supporters. Developing an engaging "pitch deck" to present your product to prospective investors instead of a business plan is a preferable alternative.

THE PITCH DECK

The pitch deck typically consists of 15 to 20 slides using PowerPoint (or another similar presentation software) and is intended to showcase the company's products, technology, and team to prospective investors.

Slides in a Pitch Deck

Your pitch deck should have slides that cover the following topics, roughly in the order laid out here, and with titles along the lines of those provided.

---

vendors who license their tools for those building products for the legal aid space, so be sure to investigate!).

2. https://www.allbusiness.com/startup-business-plan-118553-1.html.

Overview

- Summarize your "elevator pitch" here on a single slide.
- Define the mission/vision of the company.
- What do you hope to accomplish by creating this productized service? What would success look like?

The Team

- Your bio. Who are you? What is your relevant background?

The Problem

- What big problem are you trying to solve?
- To the extent possible, support this with data drawn from your research (e.g., for a tool to automate the process of residential eviction defense, include data that "90% of people facing eviction do so without any legal representation or support").

The Solution

- What is your proposed solution?
- Why is it better than other solutions or products?
- To the extent other productized services already exist in the market that arguably compete, explain why your project is significantly better.

The Market Opportunity

- How big is the addressable market?

The Product

- Give specifics on the product.
- Show slides from your prototype here and annotate special features you've developed.
- If features have been developed based on customer feedback, say so.

The Customers

- Who are the target users?
- Why will there be a big demand from them?

The Technology

- What is the underlying technology?
- How will it be maintained?

The Competition

- Who are your direct competitors, and how does your product differ?
- What indirect competitors are working in this area (e.g., humans providing "live" versions of the service you're productizing)?

Traction

- Do you have prospects for early adoption and partnerships? For example, have any interviewees pledged that their organization will pilot what you have created?

Business Model

- What is the business model?
- Will you get paid by licensing what you've created, permitting subscription-based access, receiving grants, or some other way?

The Marketing Plan

- How do you plan to market?

Financials

- What do you project it will cost to launch?
- What profits do you expect?

The Ask

- What do you want from the people listening to the pitch?
- How much money, time away from other obligations at work, or other resources are you seeking?
- Be bold here, but be prepared to support your bold ask with specific reasons why it's appropriate.

Pitch Deck DOs

Beyond the specific content, here are some other tips that will lead to a good deck.

- Do include this wording at the bottom left of the pitch deck cover page: "Confidential and Proprietary. Copyright by [Name of Company]. [Year]. All Rights Reserved."
- Do convince the viewer why the market opportunity is large.
- Do include visually interesting graphics and images.
- Do send the pitch deck in PDF format to prospective investors in advance of a meeting. Don't force the investor to get it from Google Docs, Dropbox, or some other online service, as you are just putting up a barrier against the investor actually reading it.
- Do plan to have a demo of your product as part of the in-person presentation.
- Do tell a compelling, memorable, and interesting story that shows your passion for the business.
- Do show that you have more than just an idea, and that you have gotten early traction on developing the product, getting customers, or signing up partners.
- Do have a sound bite for investors to remember you by.
- Do use a consistent font size, color, and header title style throughout the slides.

Pitch Deck DON'Ts

- Don't make the pitch deck more than 15 to 20 slides long— investors have limited attention spans.

- Don't have wordy slides.
- Don't provide excessive financial details; those can be provided in a follow-up.
- Don't try to cover everything in the pitch deck. Your in-person presentation will give you an opportunity to add and highlight key information.
- Don't use a lot of jargon or acronyms that the investor may not immediately understand.
- Don't underestimate or belittle the competition.
- Don't use a pitch deck that looks out of date. You don't put a date several months prior on the cover page. (I avoid putting a date on the cover page at all.)
- Don't have a poor layout, bad graphics, or a low-quality "look and feel." Various templates are available online at no cost; you can also, for a relatively modest cost, hire a graphic designer to make the pitch deck look more professional.

The core purpose of your pitch deck is to tell the story of how and why your idea will succeed. Beyond the need to hook a potential funding source, being able to articulate your story is important. The process of creating your pitch deck will enable you to better see any gaps in that story and to find ways to close them.

FUNDING SOURCES

Once you've created your pitch deck, you'll need to find someone to show it to. At the most basic level, the goal of a pitch deck is to persuade other people to provide whatever support you'll need to take your project to the next level. This section explores different sources of funding and different types of investors and investor-entrepreneur relationships.

Venture Capitalist Firms

Venture capital firms have arrived to invest in law. Whereas only attorneys can own law firms, that monopoly doesn't apply to legal *tech*. That means that for venture capitalists looking to invest in law, legal tech is a relatively easy avenue. Productized services (and other tools) that support law aren't law firms, and thus escape these restrictions. To put the growth of legal tech investment in perspective, in 2019, the sector took in over $1.2 billion in investment.[3] That nearly matched the total investment in legal technology startups for the seven years from 2010 to 2017. Investment has only accelerated since then, and multiple funds now exist specifically focused on investing in legal tech.

VC firms tend to invest in a specific subset of businesses—specifically, they invest in startups they believe have high growth potential. The metrics these firms use to make these determinations include number of employees, annual revenue, scale of operations, as well as the potential for these things among new operations. In exchange for their investment of money, they get equity and, with that, some measure of control over the company (this can be a blessing or a curse).

There are hundreds of online resources for understanding how VC firms analyze the viability of an investment, and if you are considering taking this route, it's important to dig in and get educated. You can do so by searching "how VC firms decide where to invest" in your favorite search engine, and you'll be pointed to dozens of insider write-ups. The good news is that the basic method for expressing your viability as a project to VCs is the one this chapter covers: the pitch deck.

Getting Meetings with Investors

There are three relatively straightforward ways to actually get in front of investors with ideas. First, a number of websites list firms and individuals looking to invest. You shouldn't have to pay anything to participate (instead, there's a "finder's fee" paid to the person who makes the connection, in this case, the website owner). The website will ask you to describe your project in general terms and invite you to share information about your goals. This basic background is shared with the investors on the roster who will, in turn, schedule a meeting if the project is something that catches their interest.

---

3. https://abovethelaw.com/2019/09/at-1-1-billion-its-already-a-record-year-for -legal-tech-investment/.

Second, dozens of pitch competitions take place every year, where people with an idea make a short presentation to a room full of other entrepreneurs and potential funders (sometimes a physical room, other times a digital room). The competition will typically announce a winner or two, and those winners get a prize, but the real prize is sharing your idea with those who might want to have a subsequent side conversation about funding it. A caveat: Some of these competitions seek to make money from new founders by charging an entrance fee. Avoid these—the competitions should be free to enter.

Finally, use your personal network. In subsequent chapters, you'll learn about promoting your idea, giving talks, and planting a flag within your community that you are working on a specific project. You can include in those conversations that you are open to discussions about funding. Like with all things marketing-related, the more work you do to spread your message, the more likely it is that an opportunity will arise from it.

Somewhere Between Venture Capital and "Bootstrapping"

There are other avenues to get your product off the ground beyond pitching your business to investors and digging into your savings. As you consider the one that best fits your needs, keep in mind that a consistent common factor is that when you take money, you're also, effectively, taking on a partner—or at least someone who is going to be entitled to look over your shoulder as you progress. It's important to recognize that you are unlikely to find "no strings" opportunities; instead, you'll need to be prepared to live with whichever organization or person becomes your funder.

Crowdfunding

The early 2000s saw the growth of crowdfunding as a means to launch a project: Bands asked their fans to help them launch a new album to sites, and sites like Kickstarter allowed hundreds of companies to build a following (and raise enough money to bring an idea to life). Crowdfunding involves raising money from a large number of people to fund a project, a company, or a cause. Sometimes, it's purely charitable, with funders making a donation. In other situations, funders receive rewards (most often these rewards are not equity, but early access, public appreciation, or the ability to buy the funded product at cost). Typically, entrepreneurs using crowdfunding set a goal amount for how much they want to raise (and provide justification for that amount), and their progress toward that goal is tracked publicly, both in terms of money paid and number of funders. If the goal isn't met, the money is typically returned to the funders. Several sites offering these services make it easy to do, and there is a cottage industry of consultants who sell services to help entrepreneurs maximize their chances of success.

Angel Investors

Think of angels as independent venture capitalists. They are typically wealthy (to be an angel investor, one must be an "accredited investor," meaning they have met certain asset requirements), but they are also unburdened by corporate investment philosophies that would prevent them from taking a risk. Angel investors are as good or as bad as the investor is. As you search sites like Angel List, look for expertise in the type of productized service you're creating and/ or the market you want to serve.

Intraprenuership

For those who already have a great job at a company that is open to it, one option is to ask for their support to launch your new venture. This can take various forms, from a partnership where the workplace takes an equity stake in exchange for start-up cash and time to work on the project; time to work on the project that would normally be spent on company business (whether a leave of absence or a portion of the work week that can be devoted to the project); or any other creative arrangement you might agree upon. One negative to this is that, unlike VCs or angel investors willing to share advice based on their past experiences, your current employer might have no such experience. It can also create strange dynamics as the project advances (if the project is a huge hit, it might mean you're less available for your traditional role; if it fails, there could be hard feelings). Finally, if you're working in a legal workplace, issues of equity can be tricky, particularly if you—or potential future investors—are not licensed attorneys.

A Note on Bootstrapping

For some, there's no need or desire to ask others for support. If you're doing this purely on your own time, with your own money, you are "boot-strapping" your idea. This means that you won't have to give up any equity or be influenced by outsiders when making decisions (of course, you *should* welcome advice from others, taken with a grain of salt, from those who have an incentive to make a quick buck from your work); you can also grow at a pace that you deem best, rather than at a rate dictated by others or the need to pay back a loan. It also means that you'll have to do without outside financial support and the advice your investors might be able to offer, and accept the likelihood of growing more slowly.

Even if you do bootstrap your idea, there are at least three good reasons why you should still go through the process of preparing a business plan.

First, regardless of who pays, you need a clear picture of how much things are going to cost and how you intend to make the books balance. In writing the business plan, you'll spell these expenses out.

Second, even if you start out bootstrapping, a time might come when you change your point of view. Perhaps things are more cost-ly than anticipated (see preceding piece of advice), or maybe you identify a way to build your product more quickly and effectively with outside support. Creating a pitch deck and having it ready will smooth that path.

Third: Re-think not asking others for support. Reid Hoffman, founder of LinkedIn, has devoted an entire book[4] to the argument that to create something great, you have to move fast to make it big. Almost always, the way to make something big and great is by seek-ing outside funding. It's certainly just one person's opinion that boot-strapping should be avoided, but that one person is worth several billion dollars based on his tech success.

Going through the process of making a pitch deck will sharp-en your business plans and force you to shake out and address

---

4. *BlitzScaling: The Lightning-Fast Path to Building Massively Valuable Companies* (Redfern, NSW, Australia: Currency Press, 2018).

unanswered questions that could kill the product down the road. It's hard, and it should be.

MAKING A BUSINESS CASE WHEN THE GOAL ISN'T PROFIT

While productization is a nice way to earn money, its key feature isn't profitability—it's scalability. In other words, the reason it can make people more money is that it allows them to offer their expertise in more than one place at once and to do so 24 hours a day, 365 days a year. But in some instances, and for some people and organizations, the goal is to serve more people, not to make more money from people.

You should still go through the process of creating a pitch deck that encapsulates your business plan. Here, though, the focus is on how your project will be a force multiplier for your organization. If, for example, you think that automating a suite of eviction defense tools will free up time for the paralegal and attorney staff, make projections about exactly how much time. Extrapolate what that will mean for the organization (e.g., "This will mean that we can process three times as many cases with no additional expense for staffing.").

Exercise: Create Your Pitch Deck

Make your own pitch deck using the guidance from this chapter.

Before you do so, spend a few minutes looking at pitch decks that launched some of the world's most famous companies. Simply search "famous pitch decks" and look through them.

You'll also find that there are various templates online that can reduce your workload. Simply search "pitch deck template." Everyone has a slightly different method, so be sure to adapt the template to your needs, guided by the one laid out in this book.

Chapter 11

Professional Responsibility and Other Special Concerns for Legal Product Makers

In 2008, Google executive Vic Gundotra's team was collaborating with Steve Jobs's people at Apple to launch a new app. Steve Jobs called Gundotra one Sunday, but Gundotra, who was participating in a religious service, did not answer his cell phone.[1] Later, when Gundotra checked his messages, he heard Steve Jobs saying, "Vic, can you call me at home? I have something urgent to discuss."

Gundotra called Jobs back.

"So, Vic," said Jobs, launching right in. "We have an urgent issue, one that I need addressed right away. I've already assigned someone from my team to help you, and I hope you can fix this tomorrow." He continued, "I've been looking at the Google logo on the iPhone, and I'm not happy with the icon. The second 'o' in Google doesn't have the right yellow gradient. It's just wrong, and I'm going to have Greg fix it tomorrow. Is that okay with you?"

Minutes later, Jobs followed up with an email to Gundotra with the subject heading: "Icon Ambulance," followed by more information for fixing the yellow tone of the second "o" in "Google."

Among other things, Steve Jobs was famous for his attention to aesthetic detail. To Jobs, the yellow in the second "o" mattered. When

---

1. https://latimesblogs.latimes.com/technology/2011/08/google-vic-gundotra-steve-jobs.html.

creating a new product for the legal field, you will encounter a host of choices. Some will be as subtle as the color tone of an "o," but rarely will your focus be aesthetic.

When it comes to developing productized services for the legal field, you will have some unique ethical responsibilities specific to your project that will factor into many of your decisions. This chapter introduces some of the unique ethical responsibilities of legal professionals. It also looks at how the ownership models of law firms create some special issues to consider during the process of building a productized service.

As you read this chapter, remember, I am not your lawyer, so any guidance I provide in this chapter should not be received as legal advice. The rules of professional responsibility are both local and nuanced; a general understanding of legal ethics principles won't be enough for you to make informed decisions regarding your specific project. This chapter is intended to give you a starting point for thinking through the types of issues and considerations you need to keep in mind. You should consult an attorney with specific questions.

LEGAL ETHICS AND PROFESSIONAL RESPONSIBILITY

There are three issues of legal ethics to be aware of when building a productized service:

1. Whether the product gives legal advice;
2. Whether an attorney-client relationship exists; and
3. Whether attorney advertising rules apply to what you've launched.

These rules differ from jurisdiction to jurisdiction, so be sure to check locally. It's also worth investigating whether your local bar association/licensing authority has released any guidance on this. When in doubt, assume that whatever guidance is out there is going to be protectionist toward brick-and-mortar law firms and attorneys and that you'll potentially get pushback if you cut into their business.

ISSUES SPECIFIC TO PRODUCTS PROVIDING LEGAL ADVICE

Lawyers giving clients legal advice are obligated to do so in a way that reflects their knowledge and takes into account their clients' needs to resolve the matter at hand. But this relationship gets complex when products replace attorneys: Can a flowchart in a book guiding a legal decision replace a lawyer? What about an app that encodes that flow chart into software? If a lawyer provided that logic to the app, are they responsible for negative outcomes that might result?

These are murky waters in American law, and they create a certain level of risk for those creating productized legal services.

The Law Only Allows Licensed Attorneys to Provide Legal Advice

Across the US, it's illegal to give legal advice unless you have a license to practice law. So, if you're creating an app or developing software to provide legal advice in some form, be aware of the potential to run afoul of the law. Bar regulators in many states keep the rules very tight about offering legal assistance in any way, shape, or form.

Legal tech creators typically anticipate this issue by including a disclaimer that clearly states that their app is not intended as legal advice and that users should be sure to consult with an attorney. But even such a caveat is no guarantee that regulators won't push back against any tech product that appears to provide legal advice.

Could the Productized Service Appear to Give Rise to an Attorney-Client Relationship?

Consider the example of an attorney in his office advising someone about the bankruptcy process. The person being advised has reason to believe that the attorney is handling their bankruptcy case; they have reason to believe that an attorney-client relationship is being formed—along with attendant expectations concerning that professional relationship, which include confidentiality, the attorney's fiduciary duty to act in the client's best interests, and the attorney's duty to handle all matters pursuant to the case with reasonable care.

But what if the exact same level of support is provided to someone through the "client's" use of an app?

In some instances, an app or productized service that helps clients can be an extension of a traditional attorney-client relationship. For example, a law firm specializing in immigration could create a document assembly tool to help their lawyers' clients fill out the appropriate forms; but the lawyers would always review the completed forms and otherwise represent the clients in the manner of a traditional attorney. In this example, the benefit of the online form is that the clients save money (in billable attorney hours). In that case, there's no reason to think the standard attorney-client relationship would be changed.

In contrast, some tools could be designed specifically and solely for self-help. The attorney who creates such tools should go through pains to make clear that no attorney-client relationship was formed or intended. As with disclaiming that online help amounts to legal advice, however, just saying there's no attorney-client relationship doesn't mean a user can't allege one exists if the matter goes wrong. The act of clearly stating that no attorney-client relationship exists will be one piece of evidence in your favor, should a user allege that one existed.

Does the Product Impact Attorney Advertising Rules?

In every state in the US, advertising rules prohibit attorneys from making any false or misleading statements about their services. If an app could potentially be seen as soliciting business for the developers or could bring business to the developers' law firm, advertising rules could (arguably) be implicated.

Consult your state's rules of professional conduct—which can be thorny.

BUSINESS AND ADMINISTRATIVE QUESTIONS

When you create a new productized service, you'll confront business challenges, too. If you work in a legal organization—whether for a firm, as an in-house attorney, or in a corporate law department—there's a chance that what you're working on is a wholly new line of business. There's also a likelihood it's the sort of project that wasn't envisioned when the organization was formed. Because of that, it's important to think about how this project might impact the organization and your role within it. In the sections below, we explore some of the business issues that you should anticipate and plan for in advance.

Drafting Website Fine Print

If it could be argued that your website product could be construed as providing legal advice, you will have to make clear what you intend users to glean from it. In most jurisdictions, an attorney-client relationship begins when an objective person in the position of the client would believe it has. One way to prevent that claim is by making clear that there is no attorney-client relationship and that you are not giving legal advice.

Privacy policies can be very tricky in the world of productized legal services. Typically, websites gather all sorts of information from users, either for their own purposes or to share or sell to third parties. If your product is helping people with legal forms or legal advice, it would seem only ethical (whether or not the regulators would say so) to keep that information secret. However, this gets tricky: If you're just providing information—not legal advice, and not within an attorney-client relationship—then the duties of confidentiality that a lawyer representing a client would typically owe don't apply.

The flipside is that, assuming there is no attorney-client relationship, the attorney-client privilege would not apply either. That means that what users load into the site may be subject to subpoena or other discovery requests in litigation. Put differently, if the productized service doesn't create an attorney-client relationship, then no one gets the benefits that flow from that relationship in terms of the ability to keep information confidential.

Making it even murkier is that even saying "there is no attorney-client relationship" in bold on your website doesn't mean a person could not argue that there was one. Courts use an "objective standard" to determine this: That is, would a reasonable person using this product believe that they were getting legal advice from someone who was their lawyer? The result is that there is no clear, dispositive way to shield oneself from this risk. The best bet is to be conservative and seek your own legal advice to create as much insulation as you—and your local legal expert—thinks is advisable.

DRAFTING TERMS—A LESSON FROM VENTURELEGALKC.COM

One of the unique challenges in building the contract shop was creating disclaimers and terms of service. To make sure that my templates weren't being openly sent around or posted, I created license terms that explained what customers can, and cannot, do with the templates they purchase. I also included disclaimers to make it clear they are buying a template, not one-on-one legal advice. I include those terms at several points in the checkout process, and I also send a link to them to each customer via email when they purchase a template.

I built these terms in as a precaution. Once someone has the Word file, there isn't much I can do to stop them from sharing it with other people. Sure, I can sue them, but that's not a great option. So I tried to make it clear up front they shouldn't share the files. So far, there's been no pushback, and people have done the right thing. It's exciting to help more people and increase my revenue at the same time.

* * *

Chris Brown is the founder of Venture Legal, which helps entrepreneurs and creative professionals with contracts and other legal needs. He also built an online contract shop where customers can purchase contract templates. The site helps people in places Chris isn't licensed, without forming an attorney-client relationship, and at a lower cost than traditional legal work. He can be reached at chris@venturelegalkc.com

---

Who Owns the Intellectual Property You're Creating?

Before using work time and resources to launch your IP project, it's worth thinking about who actually owns it. The form, the codes, the book chapter—whatever it is—even if you're the only person who directly worked on it, others can potentially claim that they should share the benefits of it. The first step is to look at your organization's current policies. It may be that your organization has an employee handbook or partnership agreement you've signed onto that addresses it. If so, you'll have to decide very early on—before you get too deep—whether it makes sense to have a conversation with supervisors and colleagues about whether to negotiate for change to the agreement to cover your project. Specifically, you need to resolve who owns the productized service you're creating.

If the agreement is silent, or one you think is worth arguing to amend, think through these questions:

- Who owns the product?
- If the product is the firm's property, what happens if you leave, retire, or are no longer able to continue the project?
- If the product needs more funding or resources (for example, hiring developers or taking time off to go on a promotional tour), who pays for it?

Insuring Against New Risks Your Product Creates

A new line of business means new risks. If, for example, your project is intended as a B2B tool to help other legal organizations more effectively track expenses, what happens if your tool breaks and miscalculates a user's numbers? If you're sued, who defends? Who pays a settlement or judgment? Malpractice coverage is typically written only to cover matters specifically related to the practice of law, and even then, sometimes only within specific practice areas. Therefore, it makes sense to contact your insurance carrier to see if your current policy covers your new, productized service. If not, consider adding coverage onto your premium to cover it. As mentioned above, you should talk, internally, about who is going to pay for the coverage, too!

Even outside of possible coverage through your malpractice carrier, other insurers offer coverage should your product lead to litigation. It's worthwhile to call an insurance agent to get a quote— they will happily describe the available coverages and the benefits of each.

* * *

Getting a product ready for market takes a great deal of thought and effort beyond just working on the product itself. Having considered and worked on some of these surrounding challenges in this chapter, it's time to get ready to launch.

Exercise: Rules Check-In

For this exercise, go to your state bar's website and see if they have created any guidance on (a) attorney advertising, (b) offering legal services online, or (c) using automated services to assist in solving legal problems.

Summarize any applicable rules, then write two to three paragraphs explaining the steps you will take to reduce the risk that your product runs afoul of them.

Chapter 12

Create a Marketing Plan for Launch

I f you've ever driven on US Interstate 95 southbound through Virginia, North Carolina, and South Carolina, you are likely familiar with strange billboards stretching along the highway for hundreds of miles.[1] Some encourage bad behavior from the passengers in the backseat—"KEEP YELLING, KIDS—THEY'LL STOP!" Some rely on silly puns—like the enormous roadside salami with the phrase, "YOU NEVER SAUSAGE A PLACE!" And still more reference Pedro, a little cartoon figure who appears to be a denizen of this mysterious location. These are signs for Pedro's South of the Border, part truck-stop, part knick-knack tourist trap off the highway in Dillon, South Carolina. At one time, more than 250 billboards advertising the store ranged from Florida to Pennsylvania.

Imagine making the long trek south (say, from New York for a week-long trip in Florida) and *not* stopping for a few minutes after seeing all of this. Impossible!

What the owners of Pedro's South of the Border have done is brilliant and unique—a piece of marketing that prepares you to buy. Lining roads with billboards in anticipation of your product launch won't likely be a good strategy for you, but making plans to get customers in the door when they cross your path is something you can be creative and strategic about.

* * *

---

1. https://matchmakerlogistics.com/2017/08/30/south-of-the-border-highway -signs/.

You are almost there. Not to the finish line—to the *start* line. The process in this book is one that can help you reimagine your professional future and build something valuable for those you serve. This chapter will help you get off on the right foot as you get into the real world by laying out a plan for marketing what you've made and being prepared to make adjustments to your product based on "live" customer feedback.

Your marketing efforts should start as early as is feasible, once you have a good sense of who your product will serve and the problem it will solve for the end user. A very soft marketing launch—in other words, when you start promoting what you're creating—can come months, or even years, before your idea is ready to go to market. This could include telling people that you're writing a book or working on an app that helps to solve a problem. (If you're sharing this information early enough, this outreach can also be used to recruit people to review prototypes and share feedback.)

As you get closer to launch, the goal is to accelerate your engagement with potential end users. Even if you have only a simple prototype of what the final product will look like, sharing that information 60 or 90 days ahead of when you plan to make the product available for purchase or use can help you gather momentum.

MARKETING

As much enthusiasm as your interview subjects, employer, and friends might have for your project, that doesn't mean your target customers will jump at it. People get a lot of advertisements and new ideas pushed at them, all of which are pitched as something that will improve their lives and their work. The reality is that what you've made is just another example of that and risks getting lost in the sea of other attention-seeking products. The good news is that, by following this book's process, you can be confident that your idea has been validated and has a real chance to catch fire.

The work of marketing is the work of spreading the message about your product. Dozens of "channels" offer different ways to reach your audience, and each has its own benefits and drawbacks.[2] To start, choose one channel and test how people respond to it.

Email Mailing Lists

Along the way, you'll talk to a lot of people — including potential customers — about your project. For each one, you should ask if it's ok to add them to your mailing list so you can send them updates and give them a try when you're ready to launch. Several companies offer free mailing list email services to smaller companies (they use a "freemium model," so it's free if you have fewer than 500 or 1,000 names; payment increases in tiers above the base number). To learn more, just search "email list management" to find the one that is right for you. The good ones offer tons of features, including easy-to-use templates to make your email visually appealing and the ability to track who clicks your message and to "segment" the list to send particular messages to certain subsets.

You need to ask permission to add people to these lists, but those who are willing are *gold*. They're likely people in your target audience who are at least somewhat interested in your product. As launch approaches, reach out to them directly and ask them to download/signup/purchase what you have created. Encourage them to forward your note to colleagues; consider offering a discount or other benefit if they do so. The goal here is to use people in your target audience to help you spread the word.

Landing Pages

A slightly more sophisticated option than just using a mailing list is to create a landing page for your product. A landing page is a website

---

2. *Traction: How Any Startup Can Achieve Explosive Customer Growth* (New York: Portfolio, 2015), by Gabriel Weinberg and Justine Mares, runs through 19 channels for building a customer base and goes into detail about how to pick the right one to start with based on your business. Here, I have focused on channels that are more accessible for those of you working on a modest budget with relatively modest technical skills.

that gives a preview of what you're working on (it can be simple — a screen shot, a short explainer video, or just plain text). Various free plug-ins allow you to collect email addresses from people who visit your web page and who want to learn more in the future or get early access to the site.

An added advantage of creating a landing page is that you can get a sense of whether you're building momentum. To do this, you simply link the landing page to Google Analytics (or a similar analytics tool), and you can track details about the traffic coming to the site. This can be a useful method when you're experimenting with different marketing channels. The information can be parsed to a far more granular level than this, too. For example, if you give a talk at your local bar association and reference your product, you can check to see whether your landing page saw a spike in traffic in the hours and days that followed.

If you're not confident of your ability to do these things on your own, there's no need to hire a web developer. Several companies — SquareSpace, Wix, and WordPress, for example — sell low-cost, fillable landing pages that integrate all of the tools described above (The world of web development has productized the creation of web design services!). If you get stuck, gig workers can set these things up to your specifications at a low cost.

Giving Talks at CLE and Other Events

Every month, I get dozens of notifications for bar association events, continuing legal education seminars, online webinars, and other events intended to help people learn more about developments in the law. I have discovered that organizers often need another person to fill out a panel or give a short talk. *You* now have something to talk about, and this is an opportunity to share your work.

The trick is not "selling from the podium." No one wants to attend a 30-minute infomercial for your specific product. However, that's not to say you can't educate others on the existence of the challenge your product solves and drive some business your way at the same time. Instead of making a sales pitch, focus your talk on the underlying problem that you solved. For example, if you built a tool to help people more efficiently apply for asylum, a talk on the problems with the current system and the reasons for it would be well-received. When it comes time to solving the problem, you should discuss all of system's problems—even those that do not involve your work in any way. Then, you could mention what you have been working on in the context of this discussion and note that you'd be happy to discuss it with anyone who is interested at the end of your presentation. The right people will find you, and you'll be building your brand in the process.

Professional Networks

If you're a member of an affinity bar group—a group for plaintiff's med-mal lawyers, or residential closing gurus—you've got a built-in community to help you test, launch, and spread the word about your idea. Reach out to this group early and often: Ask them to join your mailing list for updates, offer them beta testing slots, and tell them when you launch. This crowd is likely to be the most targeted access you'll get to your core users, so take their feedback seriously (but not *too* seriously if it's not suggestive of a pattern), and develop your project accordingly.

The Web

There's no shortage of companies and tools for purchasing ads to promote your product to very specific audiences that approximate your ideal customer. You need look no further than searching "search engine optimization consultant" or "online ad buyer" for help in this category.

EXPERT INSIGHT FROM COLIN LEVY ON SOCIAL MEDIA CADENCE

When you are on social media, people pay attention not to just to what you say, but how you say it, and how often you say it. Maintain a steady cadence to your content. Ensure that you keep putting out content on a consistent basis to ensure that your audience stays engaged. Keep in mind that

---

people's attention spans are very short—so the frequency of your content needs to address this without being overwhelming. This may take some trial and error.

* * *

Colin S. Levy is a seasoned commercial transactions lawyer as well as a prolific blogger and writer on the topics of legal innovation and legal technology. His blog can be found here: https://www.colinslevy.com/.

You can also try online marketing on your own, at no cost. Simply put, getting on social media and engaging in conversations that surround the area of your product is a starting point. Create a Twitter handle, search for terms related to your work, and try to productively engage with others having conversations about it. When appropriate, tell people about what you've made—but bear in mind that no one likes to be pitched on social media, so instead, just make yourself a part of the community. By offering others real value on social media—not selling to them but instead sharing expert insights on the topic of your product—you'll end up expanding your network and expanding your influence. This will be good for you and good for your product, too.

PREPARING TO GO VIRAL

There's a whole ecosystem of companies that make money by telling people about new start-ups. They cover new tech tools the way cable news covers politics, complete with discussion, analysis, and opinion on what's worth examining. That includes productized service offerings! Product Hunt and AngelList were two early leaders in this area. You can post your information on these sites for free, which gives other people the chance to learn more about your product idea. The potential benefit here is that your product might get picked up by reporters who want to help tell your story, or it could lead to connections with funders or others with some connection that will be helpful as you progress. New opportunities pop up regularly to share information about your product, so just do a web search for "product news" or "new product directory" when you're ready to launch and get a current list of websites where you can post. Pre-populate their forms with information about your product and be ready to hit "send" on launch day.

* * *

You're approaching the launch day for your idea-turned-product. As you gain momentum toward launching, you'll transition into a new phase. As part of that phase, you'll need to think meaningfully about how to steer the airplane after liftoff. The next chapter will prepare you for that challenge.

Exercise: Make a One-Pager

A one-pager is marketing material that advertises/demonstrates your product or service using a single page. It provides a one-page pitch of your product. You can use it as a flyer, show it as an overview to others, and use it as something to leave behind when you make your pitch.

It also includes most of the information you would ever use in telling others about your project, regardless of the channel. For that reason, creating a one-pager can be valuable because it can easily be adapted into an email, LinkedIn ad, or listserv contribution.

What to Include

- The Finished Story
  - This is a one sentence summary that tells readers the "finished story" of what they will derive from your product. Ash Maurya, in Running Lean, contrasts the "finished story" from the features and

benefits of a creation. For a resumé-building service, a feature would be "professionally designed templates"; a benefit would be "eye-catching resume that stands out"; but the "finished story" is "landing your dream job." You want to tell the finished story, then fill in the features and benefits as part of the elevator pitch.

- Your Elevator Pitch, Summarized
  - ○ Below the "finished story" headline, write out your elevator pitch so that people can understand how you'll deliver the results you've promised.
- How the Product Looks (e.g., screen grabs or pictures of the prototype)
  - ○ Use discretion here. If your product is an eBook, few people will be moved to act based on a picture of a page. By contrast, if it's a calculator or automation tool, giving people a look can add valuable context.
- Testimonials or Quotes from Users
  - ○ Only give quotes from people who have used your product if it has undergone tests that approximate the finished version that people might ultimately purchase. To the extent people giving testimonials are willing, include their name/organization. (If they are unable to permit this, you can ask if you can anonymize their identity, e.g., by referring to the person as "A Partner in the Real Estate Department of an AmLaw 200 Firm in Chicago").
- Contact Information
  - ○ Include contact information and/or information about joining your mailing list.

Before you create your one-pager, it's worth doing an Internet search for "one-pager" and taking time to look at some terrific examples. Several sites also offer free templates to create a one-pager, which reduces your need to do layout or graphic design work yourself.

Chapter 13

Launch ... and Beyond!

I remember summer nights as a child when I saw spotlights in the distance that seemed to dance in the sky and bounce off the clouds. This was suburban Boston in the 1980s, so they weren't being used to scan the skies in search of enemy aircraft. But for me, they were an invitation to adventure.

Whenever we saw them, my family would get in the car and drive to their source, with my sister and me in the back seat advising my parents where to turn to get closer to them. Invariably, we would arrive at a car dealership or restaurant, which had rented out these gigantic lights to attract visitors to their grand opening.

Since then, I've thought about just how brilliant this tactic was—an advertising and marketing channel that didn't rely on people reading the newspaper or listening to radio ads. Presumably, the spotlight machine could be rented for a few hours at relatively low cost, but it paid big dividends if it could draw in even one new customer to purchase a car. Plus, it was fun, creative, and a little irreverent.

That moment when you open for business and switch on the real or proverbial spotlights—the launch—is an important moment. It's the realization of something that has passed through a gauntlet of tests and metamorphosized from an idea to a reality. It's the end of one journey and the start of another.

This chapter is intended to help creators prepare for that moment, and the new era that follows it.

THE BIG MOMENT: THE LAUNCH

The time has finally arrived when you're ready to send a link to your new eBook to everyone on your mailing list or invite people to register for your new product or online course. This is "launch": the day that others can make use of what you've made.

On this day, it's valuable to do three things.

First, even if your product is a part-time side hustle or intended as a free resource, dedicate your entire day on the day of the launch to promoting the product. Tell your friends about it, ask your friends to tell their friends about it, Tweet about it, do interviews to post on podcasts . . . . Hit "send" on emails and posts on message boards announcing your product to the startup community. Whip up as much energy and excitement as you can to inspire people to help you get the word out.

Second, watch your analytics. Start keeping an eye on the traffic to your site, or the online sales, or whatever metric you can use to gauge whether the message is hitting home. This will be your first chance to see how end users respond, now that they can purchase or use your product for real.

Third, and finally, celebrate! This has been a long, hard process. There is still a long way to go, too, but by conceptualizing, testing, and launching a real product into the world, you've done something that very few people have accomplished. Take some time to appreciate that—both for yourself, and for the people who have sacrificed to help you achieve it. (Not too much champagne, please—you'll need to keep working hard to pick up steam, and that means staying at least somewhat focused.)

THE PRODUCT MIGHT BE LAUNCHED, BUT YOUR WORK ON IT IS NEVER *DONE*

The "what's next" after launching a new product is up to you. For some, the life of a new startup is an all-consuming experience, with every waking hour spent trying to gain momentum in terms of increased online coverage in the hopes it will lead to more product adoptions and sales revenue. For others, the new product is a small piece of what they do—a side hustle that helps them earn a few extra dollars, help others, or polish their personal brand. The direction you take is truly up to you. Here are a few considerations to think through post-launch.

Kaizen: Continuous Improvement

During the interview/prototype phase of this project, people shared their feedback with you. But like the saying goes, "Money talks." You'll have the truest indication of whether people like your productized service if they actually pay to use it. Alternatively, if it's not the sort of product people will pay for, like a free tool to help with eviction defense, then you'll define your goals differently, but you'll be able to track downloads, submissions of the form to the appropriate court, and possibly outcome metrics to show how effective it is. You'll see if more people used it this month than last month, and you'll be able to look at user feedback on whether they'd recommend it to others doing the same work. Because of that, the feedback loop of "learn, prototype, test, improve" that you used during the initial creation of your product doesn't end at launch; it's also the right way to *continue* to run your project after it launches.

Lean is a methodology to reduce waste without sacrificing productivity. Through lean management, what adds value becomes clearer as everything that doesn't add value is removed or reduced.[1] The philosophy at the core lean is *kaizen*, a Japanese word that loosely translates as "continuous improvement." In business, kaizen refers to activities that continuously improve all functions and involve all employees, from the CEO to assembly-line workers. The strength of kaizen comes from this universal participation: Everyone works to evaluate and suggest ways to improve the business. Using this approach humanizes the workplace, eliminates overly hard work, and teaches people how to spot and eliminate waste in business processes. Kaizen works well at large scale (including in industrial places, like factories with assembly lines), but you'll benefit from doing this for your project on a small scale. Advice for doing this right follows.

---

1. On this topic, check out *Lean Thinking: Banish Waste and Create Wealth in Your Corporation*, rev. ed. (New York: Free Press, 2003), by James Womack and Daniel Jones, and *The Lean Startup: How Today's Entrepreneurs Use Continuous Innovation to Create Radically Successful Businesses* (Redfern, NSW, Australia: Currency Press, 2011), by Eric Ries.

Essential Post-Launch Action Items

After launch, to set the stage for continuous improvement, you'll want to get feedback and track the way people use your product. Continue to communicate with your users — even if they don't first contact you. There are a number of easy ways to do this.

Survey Users

Survey software allows you to email all users and ask their thoughts. (Asking good survey questions is a discipline unto itself. Search online and you'll find some terrific resources to get started.) In your survey, ask open-ended questions: Use the "I like/I wish/What if" framework.

If you identify a pattern of feedback suggesting that a specific area needs improvement or change, ask about that specifically as well. Use a series of closed and open-ended questions (e.g., "Do you like the way we share links to other resources?") and if the answer is "no," follow up with more probing questions ("Would you prefer option A, B, or C to the current version?") or further open-ended questions ("How would you like to see it improved?").

Collect the information, convert it to single-sentence summaries, and review. This is the pattern you used in creating a prototype (discussed in Chapter 8), and it will help you effectively and simply decide what needs improving or changing.

Data Analytics

Use analytics software to see if you're gaining traction with users. If your project is web-based, you can add a tracker through Google Analytics to track information about the site's growth and user demographics. (Demographic information can be valuable. Information like the users' location and how they found your page can help you make smart decisions about marketing and future product developments.)

This can all be done for free, though there is a modest learning curve. (If you're uncomfortable setting it up, there's no shortage of consultants who can help you do so.)

More sophisticated analytical tools will help you see a "heatmap" of your site, so you can see what buttons people are clicking, and how long they're spending looking at specific subpages. Again, the basics can be easily set-up without professional help, but there are plenty of opportunities to outsource it.

Respond to Feedback

When feedback patterns emerge that suggest you make changes to your product, you should take the feedback seriously. Create new prototypes for the changes based on the existing work, and repeat the process of asking users if the prototype amounts to an improvement. When the feedback suggests it does, make the change. Then, begin that process again! Your job is to be constantly moving through an improvement cycle.

HOW DOCUMATE PIVOTED FROM BUILDING LEGAL PRODUCTS TO EMPOWERING OTHERS TO BUILD THEIR OWN PRODUCTS USING NO-CODE TOOLS

When I teach students how to build legal products, I don't start with document automation, templates, or design. I start with sustainability. Because, as a lawyer, I built a product that my customers loved—one that saved time and money and changed lives. But the market was small, scaling took time, customer acquisition was cost-prohibitive, and the happiest customers were those who never had to contact me again.

That product was HelpSelf, a "TurboTax for domestic violence survivors." While representing pro bono clients, the initial stages of my cases were routine and form-based: court forms for filing a domestic violence restraining order, asylum applications, and naturalization papers. These procedural tasks were based on clear rules, but they were time-consuming for pro bono attorneys, both to learn the requirements and to fill out those forms, many of which had overlapping information. So I teamed up with my engineer

---

and co-founder to build HelpSelf Legal. We spent months developing the platform, customizing the logic, accounting for each of California's 58 counties and the patchwork of local rules, and connecting to mailing and filing systems. Then, we launched it.

Our initial users, legal aid attorneys, loved it. They were able to process documents quicker and serve exponentially more clients in clinics. But to make the impact we wanted, our vision was to make this completely consumer-facing, so that our users could access the software at all hours. For our clients, domestic violence survivors, there were many reasons why coming to a legal aid attorney wasn't an option. Many didn't qualify for legal aid; others lived in rural areas, couldn't skip work, or didn't have childcare. Still more didn't have the personal and physical freedom to reach an attorney. So we thought the best way to help them would be to give them an on-demand service. What we didn't see was the barrier to giving them access to our software.

We started selling the legal workflow for $15, but that revenue was dwarfed by the cost of acquiring the customer. We were competing with family law attorneys who could pay for Google ads based on their expected $15,000 retainer for a case. To reach more people, we were slowly expanding our market to include more states, but we were faced with the challenge of researching and implementing county-specific laws, with some states having more than 200 counties. The more customers we got, the more money we were losing.

Meanwhile, people outside our target audience were noticing. Who were those people? Lawyers. We were getting tons of free press on sites like Mashable, TechCrunch, and LawSites. And the readers who reached out to us were lawyers. Their requests were all the same—"help me build what you built." So we pivoted our focus to make the tools we were using available to others. We built Documate.

Documate is a no-code platform for creating document automation and expert systems. It's what I wish I had had when building HelpSelf. Any lawyer can go onto the

Documate platform, build out their questions, add complex conditional logic, customize it with videos and images, and then connect it to their documents. These workflows can be used internally at a firm to guide lawyers and their staff. But they can also be published externally (with paywalls to collect fees), turning a law firm into a tech company.

* * *

Dorna Moini is the founder of Documate, a no-code platform for creating legal products. Prior to Documate, she was a litigator, and she currently teaches the Legal Innovations Lab at USC Law School. She can be reached at dorna@documate.org.

INVEST IN AUTOMATION

As your productized service takes off, the needs of its users will mean more work for you. Sometimes this will mean giving more customer service to troubleshoot billing problems; other times it will mean adding to your original project to meet user feedback. From the day of launch onward, you will want to look for issues that come up recurrently and seek ways to automate the solutions to them.

Unless you're in a position to reduce your role in your day job in favor of this project, you'll have to think about ways to serve more people while not taking on more than your capacity allows. Simplifying the back end of the work (things like processing payments, having an easy way to give refunds, and communicating with customers) is key. Don't release a product that makes everyone else's life run smoothly but multiplies the complexity of your own.

Automating the back end is one way to reduce the complexity of managing your product in the days and weeks following the launch. What this means will necessarily differ from product to product, but some tools will universally apply. For example, if you've committed to making ten social media posts a week to promote your product, available low-cost (sometimes free) tools can schedule the postings for you (you can do a web search for "Twitter management tools," or for Facebook or any other relevant social network). Such tools allow you to preload your language, and some will even optimize the moment of release for when they predict they'll be most likely to reach your audience.

Another useful route is to provide a "Frequently Asked Questions" link on your site. Instead of answering the same user questions over and over, you identify the most common questions and send users to your prepared responses before they email you.

THINK ABOUT GETTING OUTSIDE HELP

At some point, if things go well, you'll likely need help. That's not a bad thing, especially if you've exhausted your ability to meet demand and keep the product going on your own and you're earning enough revenue from the product to justify the expense.

That help may come in the form of another productized service that performs some of the work that you have been doing. Many services useful to those who productize services have, themselves, been turned into productized services. For example, you no longer need to hire a marketer or designer to update your site: Instead, productized services allow you to manage tasks like marketing on your own. There are also new, lower-cost opportunities for hiring actual human helpers, too, through "gig work" sites that connect small business owners with programmers and others who specialize in doing tasks associated with operating a business. These workers tend to use software to streamline their work, so they can do things efficiently and with less expense to you. For example, if you'd like to get to the top of the search results page on your favorite search engine, experts are available who, for a fee, can help you get there. They use sophisticated software to help them in the process of helping you.

When that's not enough, still other services can help get you high-level expertise at a lower cost. For example, planning the technological future of your project would have historically required hiring a chief technology officer—likely with a six-figure annual salary and demands for partial ownership—but now, a new generation of "fractional CTOs" have emerged who can advise businesses on an hourly or short-term contract basis. The person filling this role is fractional in the sense that they're doing the work part-time. They're typically paid as an independent contractor based on an agreement that entitles you to a certain portion of their time. If you've got a big project, or just need someone to be there in the background to keep an eye on the tech end of things, that's what your fractional CTO can do. They're easy to find, too, with sites like LinkedIn having hundreds of fractional CTOs who are open to taking on new clients.

The name of the game for you when deciding what to spend money on is the same as for your users: Look for places where, instead of paying full-price for a human doing some tasks that could be automated away, you can pay a fraction of the price for automated tools with a human expert available as a safety net or to offer sophisticated judgments that software can't.

YOU BUILT A KILLER PRODUCT, YAY! NOW MAKE SURE IT DOESN'T DIE.

I love building products that are well-designed to meet a really important need. I hate. hate. hate. building products that don't thrive.

My team is very good at building products that are designed to meet a particular user need, in large part because we care about getting it right. By "right," I mean —

1. The right product,
2. For the right user,
3. That solves the right problem,
4. In the right way.

But here's a secret:

That perfect product is constantly on the precipice of death. It is ready for you to neglect it in one of several common ways so that it can live out the rest of its life as a zombie project—one that exists-ish, but no one is using it, no traffic is being driven to it, no content is being updated or added, and it is broken due to browser updates and a lack of maintenance.

You may have heard the phrase "software is never done." It's a dumb phrase, particularly outside the SaaS context. Software can be "done" in the sense that you have a product out that is delivering value. But even if it's done, it still needs to be maintained. People still need to learn that it exists. People need to be able to use it without it breaking. Once those things no longer happen, your *done* product be *dead*.

How do we avoid such untimely and devastating deaths? A sustainability plan can definitely help.

WHAT'S IN A SUSTAINABILITY PLAN?

In offering this rundown of sustainability planning, I'm making a few assumptions about you, the reader:

1. You're building a product that is not the core mission of your business (i.e., you're not a tech company); and
2. You're building a product that is not designed to create a robust new revenue stream.

For our clients that have engaged us to build a product that is going to substantially impact their business, make them money, or is otherwise core to the organization's goals, sustainability is more naturally a focus with motivation to sustain baked in.

For the rest of you, here is what you need to consider well before your team writes a line of code (and indeed, best to consider before you even write that grant application, seek funding from leadership, or write an RFP).

BASIC MAINTENANCE

You cannot expect to be done paying developers after a public launch of your product. Unless you're actively testing and iterating, though, it's going to be substantially less than what you're paying for active build. Your budget for basic maintenance just cannot be $0 (which is often a reality for grant-funded projects). At an absolute minimum, you should have someone doing a run through the application once a month to check for bugs that might have cropped up due to browser changes, reviewing documentation on technologies underlying the product to be alert for security patches, etc. Extra points for you if you include budget for continued chipping away at your backlog.

MARKETING

Your app may be super awesome, but it matters little if no one learns about it. From the very beginning, you need to budget for ongoing marketing. You cannot rely on PR you may receive after the launch of the product to propel users to your site. Chances are, the users you're targeting will not ever see those articles. If your organization doesn't have internal marketing that knows how to market digital products, engage an outside marketing team, and do it early. This is important so that you get a sense of an ongoing budget for marketing post-launch, which can be substantial.

CONTENT

There are very few applications in the legal realm without an important content component. I'm using content quite broadly here to refer to any blog-style articles about a legal issue, information in a product about legal rights and obligations, forms, question flow content, etc.

No matter if you are a non-profit or a massive law firm, the content is used to educate users, promote some action, etc. And if that content is old or . . . wrong . . . the product can end up doing more harm than good. At best, it can harm the perceived trustworthiness of your application and/or organization, at worst it can actually cause legal harm to your users.

Content for products we build is often created by people who have other very demanding day jobs. In the law firm context, associates are usually roped into creating content. In the non-profit world, volunteer lawyers or organization staff are brought in to create content. This method is possibly sustainable through the development and launch of a product, but long-term content needs to be someone's job. Or at least a well-defined part of someone's job. This obviously comes with cost.

MORE THAN ONE CHAMPION

Often, to get a project through an organization, there is one person who is committed and dedicated to the success of a project. There is benefit in having an internal "product owner" who makes the project their priority, but it sets up the possibility for a challenging situation. What if that person leaves the organization? What if, after launch, they get pulled back into other duties? We see this as a common cause for products fizzling out. Products need more than one champion.

None of this work is worthwhile if you don't plan for long-term sustainability. We've seen way too many good products go to waste due to a lack of planning.

I know a lot of people that read this are invested in the use of technology to improve the way people experience the law. There's a lot of good work going on out there, let's work harder to be sure that that work is having the impact we all desire.

* * *

Nicole Bradick is the Founder and CEO of Theory & Principle, a company focusing on product design and development in the legal and justice space. She can be reached at nicole@theoryandprinciple.com.

CLOSING UP SHOP

Following the method this book lays out maximizes the chances your productized service will succeed. It doesn't guarantee it, though.

A few signs that it's time to return to the drawing board and suspend the project you're working on:

- You're out of passion.
- You're out of money, time, or other resources.
- You're out of ideas for how to change things to improve the product.

Even if you do shut down operations, however, a time may come when you want to bring it back—the law changes, markets change, society changes. Perhaps you were just too far ahead of your time. For that reason, you should spend a bit of time before closing up to write out your thoughts on what you've learned, what challenges you couldn't surmount, and any other details about the project's operation that you might need if you picked it up again in a few years or gave it to someone else to do so.

This is never a fun thing, but if you do it with the right mindset it can make your product's unwanted outcome an easier pill to swallow. Think of yourself as a scientist, applying the scientific method. You have a hypothesis about what will happen in a given experiment, but proving it requires actually running it. Sometimes your hypothesis will be proven; other times it won't. Either way, you've learned something. You've also gained insights for regrouping and testing your next hypothesis with a bit more accuracy.

FINAL THOUGHTS

One of my law practice mentors was fond of saying "A case should have a beginning, a middle, and an end." Books, too. Productized services, however, don't need to have an end. After launch, my hope and wish for you is that this process helped you create a real thing that lives in the real world and benefits real people (including you!). If your goal was to make money, I hope it does that for you, too. If the goal was to help more people get access to legal help, I hope it meets that goal.

If—when—your project takes off, you'll have a series of other challenges: how to balance its success with the needs of your current job, when to launch your *next* big idea using the method you've learned in this book, how to deal with competition that arises. These things are well beyond the scope of this book, but, no doubt, there will be people and resources to help you solve them.

Of real importance beyond your product itself is that the exercise of creating it changes your relationship with your work, your colleagues, and your clients. It's my sincere hope that the lessons this book imparts permeate your entire professional life. This book is merely a productization of the classroom-style teaching I have dedicated my career to, and your success in growing is the metric of success most important to me.

I hope this book started you on your journey.

Exercise: Reflect

Creating products — or creating virtually anything complex — is an iterative process. You make a version, test it, then use that information to improve the next version of it.

For your final exercise, write out at least three things that following the process in this book taught you that will stay with you for future use, even if the underlying productized service you created does not succeed.

Epilogue

At the moment that I am writing these words, I am self-isolating with my family at home. It's spring 2020, and coronavirus is sweeping the world, including my corner of it just outside of Boston, Massachusetts. Most things are shut down, including access to the courts in almost all circumstances.

This crisis has put people, particularly those without financial means, in an even worse position in getting access to justice than before. At the outset of the pandemic, the wonderful Chief Justice of my state's supreme court, Ralph Gants, sent a letter encouraging legal professionals to find ways to continue to provide legal assistance during the pandemic — to improvise and be creative in proposing solutions to the problem of limited access to legal services in the shadow of a pandemic.[1] I want to share two stories about the bookends of why this has become so important and how it presents a shining opportunity for change.

In early 2020, in the immediate run-up to the COVID-19 lockdown, mortgage interest rates were historically low. As a homeowner with a mortgage, I leapt at the chance to refinance my home. At little cost, I calculated the reduced mortgage rate would save my family tens of thousands of dollars over its term, and even shorten the term of the mortgage. I found a bank willing to offer a great rate and began the refinancing process. In typical fashion, the application took several months, and was to culminate with an in-person closing. About two weeks before the closing date, my kids' schools closed because of safety concerns. Five days before the closing, the entire state of New York went on lockdown. I called the bank and asked if we could postpone the closing until this state of emergency had passed. The loan officer said we had to close on schedule because they already sold the mortgage to an investor and that deal would fall through

---

1. Sadly, Chief Justice Gants passed away in September 2020. His death was a profound loss for the legal community and those committed to access to justice for all.

if we didn't. I next called the law firm handling the closing for the bank. I explained my wife and I had two young children. Since we both needed to sign for the refinancing, they would have to come with us. I explained that, particularly with children involved, we preferred not to leave the house, let alone bring them into a law office. While the attorneys were sympathetic, they explained that they were unable to do the deal remotely because they weren't set up for it. We had to come in.

We drove with our kids to the law firm and parked in the lot. We took turns masking up and going into the office to sign papers. When I first entered the offices, I saw that the closing attorney, in a mask and blue surgical gloves, had just finished using Clorox to spray all the chairs, the desk, and even the papers for us to sign. As he handed me a pen, he assured me that it was brand new—right out of the box. I felt badly for him: We only had to do this once, but he would have to oversee many more closings that day, as well as in the days following. I signed my name on the documents as fast as he could put them in front of me, washed my hands, and returned to the car, where I hung out with the kids while my wife went in to repeat the paper-signing process.

We spent most of the ride home thinking about how backward it all seemed. Our local rules allowed every step in this process to happen remotely, except for the notarization (for which we could have gone to our neighbor, a notary (and those rules are changing fast, too).

If the law office that had handled our closing been savvy to legal tech, imagine how their work would change: Instead of renting a large office staffed by a receptionist and stocked with expensive copiers, attorneys could conduct an entire closing by video conference. Instead of printing and assembling reams of paper, paralegals could insert variables into a document assembly tool and deliver the files to an attorney for review.

For us as consumers, if the closing law firm had used legal tech effectively, we wouldn't have had to drive 30 minutes each way for a 20-minute closing. Instead, my wife and I could have logged into a video conference and e-signed all the closing documents while an attorney recited the disclosures. We also wouldn't have had to expose our family to an unsafe situation during a deadly pandemic.

So that's an example of "this ought to change." At the other end of the spectrum, and in response to Chief Justice Gants's challenge, my colleagues at the Suffolk University Law School Legal Innovation & Tech Lab immediately swung into action productizing services at the start of the pandemic. The Lab, which I co-founded (picturing rosier use-cases than this for its team), organized teams of students and outside volunteers to automate forms that would help keep the justice system running. Our Lab's leaders, David Colarusso and Quinten Steenhuis, oversaw about 100 people working from around the globe to develop a streamlined process for generating high-quality tools to address the most pressing needs of the justice system. They deftly cut through courts' red tape and arranged for forms once hand-filed to be accepted electronically. As laws changed, they updated their software in response. Their efforts helped ensure that people would continue to have access to important legal services every day for fighting evictions, handling family law matters, and defending consumer debt claims.

Beyond Suffolk Law, legal tech companies like Documate and Afterpattern (which create no-code automated documents), LawDroid (which provides a suite of legal automation tools), and others have also lent a hand by expanding access to their legal service products and lowering their paywalls. They have the ability to quickly and remotely create innovative tools that can do the work of lawyers, helping to fill the breach in times of social distancing.

This text explores new and innovative ways to deliver legal services as an alternative to traditional methods that are less efficient or more expensive. We have seen how traditional modes of service can flag or break in a crisis. The alternatives covered in this book are not only economical and efficient, but they may also provide an access to justice lifeline where traditional methods cannot.

Index

CPSIA information can be obtained
at www.ICGtesting.com
Printed in the USA
LVHW081514131021
700336LV00010B/818

9 781543 835175